The ChatgPt-5 Millionaire

The Complete 5 in 1 Collection

Master AI to Build Passive Income, Automate Your Business, and Achieve Financial Freedom Using ChatGPT-5

GRAPEVINE BOOKS

Published by

GRAPEVINE BOOKS

www.grapevinebooks.com

email: contact@grapevinebooks.com

Ordering Information:

Quantity sales: Special discounts are available on quantity purchases by corporations, associations, and others.

For details, reach out to the publisher.

First published by Grapevine Books, 2025

CONTENTS

Get Your Free E-book

Get Your Free E-book
Scan the QR code below to instantly access the e-book
'The ChatGPT-5 Money Map: Exactly What to Ask AI at Each Stage of Wealth Buildiing', absolutely free

SCAN ME

https://bonus.grapevinebooks.com/aimoneymap

Introduction

Let me give you the most valuable sentence in this book before you have spent a single hour on it: nobody is going to hand you a million dollars for owning a ChatGPT subscription.

If that costs me the sale, so be it. But I do not think it will, because you already suspected it. You have seen the posts promising passive riches by Friday. You have watched someone wave a screenshot and a course link. Some part of you knew it was too clean. That instinct is correct, and it is the most useful thing you own going into this. Hold on to it.

Here is what is actually true, and it is bigger than the hype, not smaller. Something rare has happened. The cost of producing work that people pay for has collapsed. Writing, design, research, code, analysis, customer support, the things companies and people spent real money on for decades, can now be produced by one person, working alone, at a speed and quality that used to take a team. That is a genuine shift in who gets to play. It is not a lottery ticket. It is a tool that quietly removes the barriers that used to keep ordinary people out of high-value work.

The difference between this book and the others is simple. I am going to show you the math, the methods, and the places where it breaks. I will tell you what works, what it costs in real effort, and where most people quietly fail. You will not find income screenshots in here, because screenshots prove nothing and you know it. You will find a system you can actually run.

Who this book is for. You can already use ChatGPT. You can open it, type, and get something useful back. That puts you past the starting line, and this book respects that. I am not going to spend forty pages teaching you what a chatbot is. I am going to spend the book teaching you how to turn the tool you already have into income. If you are newer to AI, you are still welcome here. Wherever a term might trip you up, you will find a short PLAIN ENGLISH note that catches you up in one line and lets you keep moving.

How the book is built. It is five books in one, and they are not five separate topics stapled together. They are five stages of one journey, a ladder you climb in order. Book One sets the operating model so you stop thinking like a user and start thinking like an operator. Book Two gets you earning with services, because cash now beats theory later. Book Three turns what you learn into products that sell without your time. Book Four automates the machine so it does not depend on you being awake. Book Five is about stacking those pieces into something that adds up to real freedom, defined honestly.

How to use it. Read it in order the first time. Each rung assumes the one below it. At the end of most chapters there is a TRY THIS box with a small action. Do them. The readers who make money are not the ones who read fastest. They are the ones who close the book and go do the thing.

One more thing. As you read, you will notice I rarely name a specific model version in the methods. That is on purpose. The tools will keep changing names and numbers. The thinking in this book is built to outlast all of it, so the book stays useful long after today's model is yesterday's news.

Your free bonus, including every prompt and template referenced inside, is waiting for you. Details are on the next page. Grab it now so you have it open while you read.

Let's begin where every honest version of this has to begin: with the math.

What is ChatGPT-5.5 and Why It Changes Everything

You are living in the middle of a technology shift that is bigger than the invention of the internet. Artificial Intelligence is not just a trend. It is the next stage of how humans work, create, and earn money. And at the heart of this revolution is ChatGPT-5.5. If you are serious about building wealth, creating a lifestyle of freedom, and staying ahead of the crowd, you need to understand why this version of ChatGPT changes everything.

But first, let us understand what Artificial Intelligence is.

Artificial Intelligence (AI) is a computer system that can think, learn, and make decisions in ways that once required human intelligence. It is not magic, although it might feel like it the first time you see it create a detailed business plan in seconds. AI uses large amounts of data to recognize patterns, make predictions, and generate useful results.

Over the last few years, AI tools have moved from research labs into the hands of everyday entrepreneurs. And now, with ChatGPT-5.5, you have access to an AI that can do more than just answer questions. It can become your business partner, content creator, market researcher, and personal strategist all in one.

When ChatGPT-3 first arrived in 2020, it was met with equal parts excitement and skepticism. People marveled at its ability to write emails, answer questions, and mimic human conversation, yet many saw it as a fun experiment rather than a business essential. Early adopters used it to draft blog posts or brainstorm ideas, but most businesses stayed on the sidelines, unsure of how to integrate it into real operations.

The technology was impressive for its time, but it had limitations. The answers could be generic, the reasoning basic, and the accuracy inconsistent. In those days, AI tools felt more like digital party tricks than reliable partners in productivity.

By 2023, ChatGPT-4 changed the conversation entirely. The leap in comprehension and accuracy was dramatic. This version could hold context across longer conversations, deliver nuanced explanations, and adapt to different tones of voice. Suddenly, AI was not just a toy. Entrepreneurs began using it to produce marketing copy, draft sales emails, generate course outlines, and even help with coding tasks.

Industries started to take notice. Real estate agents used it to write listing descriptions in minutes. Coaches relied on it to brainstorm workshop content. E-commerce sellers generated product descriptions that matched their brand voice. The shift was clear: AI was moving from optional helper to core business tool.

From ChatGPT-3 to ChatGPT-5.5: Why This Upgrade Matters

Now, with ChatGPT-5.5, the transformation is complete. This is no longer about getting a "good enough" draft. It is about building entire workflows around AI. ChatGPT-5 is faster, more accurate, and capable of advanced reasoning that makes it useful for planning strategy, not just creating content.

One of the most powerful advancements is multimodal capability. ChatGPT-5 can process and generate text, images, and data in the same conversation. You can upload a spreadsheet of sales numbers, ask for trends, and receive a written summary along with visual charts. You can feed it an image and request a matching blog post. These features save hours of work that previously required multiple tools and team members.

ChatGPT-5.5 also learns your preferences better. With brand style guides and persistent memory features, it can consistently write in your tone, reference your past projects, and align with your business goals. This personalisation means you spend less time editing and more time executing ideas.

The journey from ChatGPT-3 to ChatGPT-5.5 shows a clear pattern: AI tools are becoming not just useful, but indispensable. For entrepreneurs, the implications are enormous. What once required a small team can now be done solo with AI support. Speed to market has shortened from months to days. Marketing, customer service, product development, and research can all be streamlined with a single tool.

The competitive advantage is no longer in whether you use AI, but how well you integrate it. Those who treat it as a strategic partner will outpace those who see it as a novelty. Just as businesses that embraced the internet early gained a decade-long head start, those adopting AI at a deep level now are setting themselves up for long-term dominance.

When ChatGPT-3 first appeared, people were amazed at how it could write emails, essays, and marketing copy in seconds. ChatGPT-4 took it further with better reasoning, deeper knowledge, and a more natural writing style. Now ChatGPT-5.5 is here, and the difference is like upgrading from a bicycle to a high-speed train.

Here is what makes ChatGPT-5 a leap forward:

1. **Advanced Reasoning** – It can solve complex problems, create step-by-step strategies, and adapt its answers to your exact goals.

2. **Massive Knowledge Base** – It draws on a wider range of updated information, giving you more accurate and relevant insights.

3. **Multi-Modal Capabilities** – It can work with text, images, and data inputs, opening doors to new creative and business uses.

4. **Personalization** – It can learn your style, remember your preferences, and produce content that feels uniquely yours.
5. **Speed and Efficiency** – It produces better results faster, saving you hours of work every week.

Chapter 1
The Real Opportunity (and the Honest Math)

There are two ways to enter this field, and they lead to completely different outcomes.

The first way is to chase the promise. You buy the dream of money that arrives while you sleep, you collect prompts and tools, you wait for the income to start, and when it does not, you blame the tool and move on to the next shiny thing. This is the path most people take. It is also the path that produces the angry one-star reviews and the abandoned side projects. I want you off it before the end of this chapter.

The second way is to understand the machine. Once you see clearly where money actually comes from, and what AI does and does not change about it, the fog lifts. You stop hunting for secret tricks and start doing the small number of things that work. That is the path of the operator, and it is the only one I know that compounds.

So let's build the machine in plain sight.

Where money actually comes from

Strip away every guru phrase and money obeys one boring equation. You make money when you deliver something of value to someone who wants it and is willing to pay. That is it. Write it out and it looks like this:

`What you earn = (what the result is worth to the buyer) × (how many buyers want it) − (what it costs you in time and money to deliver)`

Read that again, because every strategy in this entire book is just a different way of moving one of those three terms. There is no fourth lever. Anyone selling you a fourth lever is selling you a story.

> **KEY IDEA** Money is value delivered to a willing buyer, minus your cost to deliver it. Every method in this book moves one of those three numbers. Nothing moves a number that is not in the equation.

Now watch what AI does to it.

What AI changes, and what it refuses to change

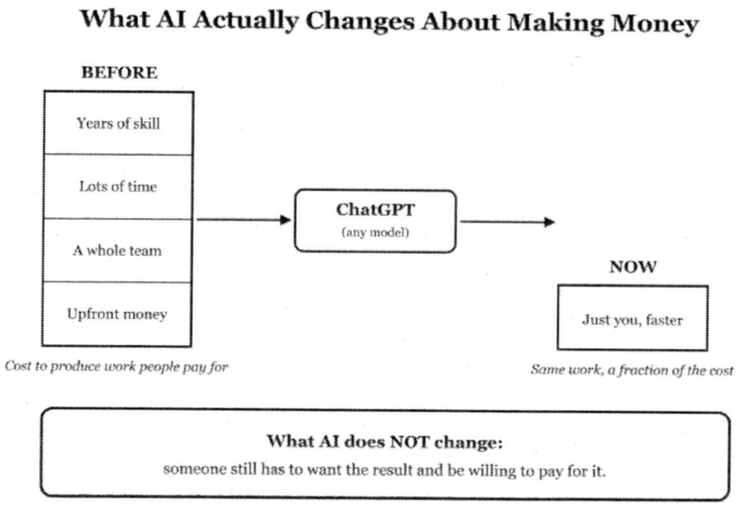

Look at that last term in the equation, the cost to deliver. For most of history, that number was the wall that kept ordinary people out of high-value work. Producing a professional article, a polished design, a working piece of software, a researched report, took years of skill, hours of labor, often a whole team, and real money up front. That wall is why most people sold their time by the hour instead of selling results.

AI takes a sledgehammer to that wall. The work that used to need a team and a week can now come from one person in an afternoon. Your cost to deliver drops through the floor. This is the real opportunity, and it is enormous. It is the first time in a long time that a single motivated person can produce, at quality, the kind of output that used to require a payroll.

AI also nudges the middle term. Because you can produce more, faster, you can serve more buyers than you could alone. One person can now run the output of several.

But here is the part the hype skips, and it is the most important sentence in the chapter. AI does almost nothing to the first term, and nothing at all to whether demand exists. It does not make a worthless result valuable. It does not create buyers who were not there. You can generate a thousand articles nobody wants in an afternoon, and a thousand times zero is still zero.

REALITY CHECK "AI will make you money." No. AI lowers the cost of producing work. That is a multiplier, and a multiplier on zero is zero. If you point a cheap production engine at something nobody wants, you produce worthlessness very efficiently. The money is not in the AI. It is in pointing the AI at something people already pay for.

This single distinction separates the people who earn from the people who buy books like this and never see a dollar. The winners do not ask "how do I make money with AI." They ask "what do people already pay for that I can now deliver far cheaper and faster than the people charging for it today." Those are completely different questions, and only one of them has an answer.

The most misunderstood word in this entire field

Passive.

Your title has the word in it, my book's spine is built around it, and your buyers came looking for it, so let me be straight about what it actually means, because the fantasy version has wrecked more beginners than any other idea here.

Passive income is real. It is also earned. Every passive income stream that lasts was built by someone who did concentrated, active work up front, creating an asset, then set it up to sell or run with little ongoing effort. The income is passive. The building was not. The fantasy sells you the second half and hides the first. This book sells you both halves, in order, which is exactly why it works.

PLAIN ENGLISH An "asset," in this book, is anything you build once that can earn more than once: a product, a template, a system, an audience. Trading hours for money is not an asset. Building something that sells while you sleep is.

That is why we earn with services first and build passive products second. Services give you cash, proof of what people will pay for, and the raw material you later turn into assets. Skipping straight to "passive" is like trying to collect rent on a house you have not built yet.

The hype version and the honest version

Here is the field, laid out plainly. The left column is what gets sold. The right column is what is true. Keep this table in mind every time you see an ad for someone else's course.

The hype says	The honest version
Make money passively in minutes	Build an asset actively first, then it can earn passively

No skills needed, anyone can do it	You need one skill the market wants; AI multiplies it, it does not replace it
AI does all the work for you	AI does the production; you do the judgment, the selling, and the quality control
Just use these magic prompts	Prompts are tools, not a business; the business is value and demand
The first mover gets rich	The clear, reliable operator gets paid, early or late
Quit your job immediately	Earn on the side until the income is real, then decide from strength

Notice that the honest column is not discouraging. It is more hopeful than the hype, because it is achievable. You do not have to be first, lucky, or technical. You have to be useful and consistent. That is a bar you can actually clear.

How this book gets you from here to real income

The whole journey is a ladder with three rungs. You will spend a full book on each, but here is the shape so you always know where you are standing.

Rung	What you do	What it gives you	What it costs
1. Services (Books One and Two)	Sell a result you deliver with AI	Cash now, and proof of real demand	Your time, per job
2. Products (Book Three)	Package what you repeat into something sellable	Income that is no longer tied to your hours	Active building up front
3. Automation (Books Four and Five)	Systematize and stack the streams	A business that runs without you in every step	Effort to build the systems once

You climb in order for a reason. Rung one funds and de-risks everything above it. By the time you build a product in rung two, you already know what people pay for, because they paid you for it in rung one. By the time you automate in rung three, you have something worth automating. People who jump straight to rung three automate a business that does not exist yet. That is the most common expensive mistake in this whole space, and you are going to skip it.

REALITY CHECK "Start with passive products, that's where the money is." It is where the money ends up, not where it starts. A product is a bet on what people want. After rung one, you are not betting. You already know, because they paid you. Earning first is not the slow path. It is the path that does not waste six months building something nobody buys.

The real difference between earners and readers

I will end the chapter with the most uncomfortable truth in it, because it is also the most freeing.

The thing standing between you and income is almost never knowledge. It is rarely the right prompt, the right tool, or the right model. By the end of this book you will have more method than you need. The thing that decides whether you earn is whether you narrow your focus to one thing and ship it to a real person who can say yes or no.

Most readers will finish this book, feel informed, and do nothing, because doing nothing is safe and shipping something invites rejection. The earners are the ones who tolerate that discomfort. They pick one skill, build one offer, send it to one potential buyer, and learn from the answer. Then they do it again. That loop, run a hundred times, is the entire game. Everything else in this book exists to make that loop faster and more profitable.

So before you turn the page, do the one thing that puts you on the operator's path instead of the dreamer's.

TRY THIS Take five minutes and write down three things you can already do that someone, somewhere, pays money for. Not what you are passionate about. What people pay for. Writing, organizing, explaining, designing, researching, fixing, teaching, selling, anything. Do not filter for "is this a business." Just list three. This is the raw material we point your new, cheap production engine at in the next chapter. Keep the list where you can see it.

In Chapter 2, we make the shift that makes all of this work: moving from someone who uses ChatGPT to someone who operates it for profit. The tool stays the same. What changes is the person holding it.

Chapter 2
From User to Operator
(The Mindset Shift That Pays)

Two people sit down at the same screen, open the same ChatGPT, and type into the same box. One of them will make money with it. The other will not. The tool is identical. The difference is entirely in the person.

That difference has a name, and this chapter is about crossing it. On one side is the user. On the other is the operator. You already know how to use ChatGPT, which means you are a competent user, and that is exactly why this chapter matters: being a good user is the thing most likely to keep you from becoming an operator, because it feels like enough. It is not enough. It is the floor.

Let me show you the gap, then show you how to cross it.

The user and the operator

A user goes to ChatGPT with a question and leaves with an answer. The transaction lives and dies inside the chat window. The user is the consumer of the output. They ask it to explain something, draft something, brainstorm something, and then they read it, nod, and close the tab. The value, whatever there was, stayed with them.

An operator goes to ChatGPT with a deliverable in mind and leaves with something a third person will pay for. The chat window is not the destination. It is a workshop. The operator is not the consumer of the output. They are the producer of a result that leaves the building and lands in front of a buyer. The user asks "can you help me understand email marketing." The operator asks "what does a client need delivered, and how do I use this tool to deliver it better and faster than the person they would otherwise hire."

> **KEY IDEA** A user consumes ChatGPT's output. An operator sells it. The whole shift is learning to point the tool outward, at a buyer, instead of inward, at yourself.

Here is the same person, before and after the shift, across the things that actually decide income.

Dimension	The user	The operator
Goal	Get an answer	Deliver a result someone pays for
The chat window is	The destination	A workshop
Role they play	Consumer of output	Director of production

What they bring	A question	Context, judgment, a quality bar
First draft is	The finished thing	A starting point to refine
When output is wrong	They accept it or give up	They diagnose and correct it
What they end up with	Something they read	Something they ship
How they treat a good result	Move on	Save the recipe and reuse it

Read down the operator column and you will notice none of it is technical. Not one row requires you to understand how the model works. It requires you to act like a professional who happens to direct an extremely fast, occasionally unreliable production assistant. Which is exactly what you now are.

You are the director, not the laborer

Think of ChatGPT as the most capable, fastest, and least judgmental worker you have ever managed. It will produce a first draft of almost anything in seconds. It never complains and never tires. It is also confidently wrong on a regular basis, has no idea what your buyer actually needs unless you tell it, and has no taste of its own.

That description should tell you precisely what your job is. You are not the laborer anymore. The laborer is sitting in the box, working for free, around the clock. Your job is the work that the laborer cannot do: deciding what to make, telling it exactly what "good" means, catching what it gets wrong, and standing behind the result with your name on it. That is the work that has value, and notice that it is the work AI cannot take from you. The fear that "AI will replace me" belongs to the user. The operator owns the parts of the job that have no AI substitute.

> **REALITY CHECK** "AI is going to replace people like me." It replaces the part of the work that was always going to be commoditized: raw production. It does not replace judgment, taste, accountability, or the relationship with the person paying. Operators do not get replaced by AI. Users who refuse to become operators get out-competed by the ones who did.

The single skill that separates the two: the brief

If you take one practical skill from this chapter, take this one. The gap between a user and an operator is mostly the gap between a question and a brief.

A user types a question. A brief is what a professional gives a contractor: the context, the goal, the audience, the constraints, the format, an example of what good looks like, and the standard it will be judged against. The same model produces mediocre work from a question and excellent work from a brief, because you stopped making it guess.

PLAIN ENGLISH A brief is a set of instructions complete enough that a competent stranger could do the job without asking you a single follow-up question. If you would have to explain more to a human freelancer, you have to explain it to the AI too.

Watch the difference on a single task.

The user types: *Write a blog post about email marketing.*

What comes back is generic, because the request was generic. Garbage in is not even the right phrase. Vagueness in, vagueness out.

The operator briefs it instead:

- **Role:** You are a direct-response copywriter who writes for busy small business owners.
- **Audience:** Owners of small online stores who already send some email but get poor open rates and do not know why.
- **Goal:** A 900-word post that gets the reader to try exactly one tactic this week. One. Not ten.
- **The one tactic:** Improving the subject line, with a simple before-and-after method they can copy.
- **Constraints:** Plain language, no marketing jargon, short paragraphs, no filler intro. Assume they are skeptical and short on time.
- **Format:** A hook in the first two lines, three short sections with headers, one clear action at the end.
- **Quality bar:** A real store owner should finish it and be able to write a better subject line in the next ten minutes. If a sentence does not help them do that, cut it.

Same tool. Same thirty seconds of generation. A completely different result, one you could put in front of a paying client. The operator did not write the post. The operator made it possible for the tool to write a good one. That is the job.

The operator never ships the first draft

A user reads the first output and treats it as finished. This is the single fastest way to destroy your reputation in this business, and it is worth saying plainly because so many people learn it the expensive way.

AI output is a draft. Always. It is a strong, fast draft, often eighty percent of the way there, and that last twenty percent is the entire difference between something a client values and something they recognize instantly as cheap AI filler. Buyers can smell raw output now. They have seen enough of it. The moment they sense it, your price collapses and your referrals stop.

So the operator does three things to every draft before it leaves the building: reads it as the buyer would, fixes what is generic or wrong, and adds the specific judgment the AI could not have, the detail that proves a thinking human was in the loop. This is the JUDGE and REFINE step, and it is where your value actually lives.

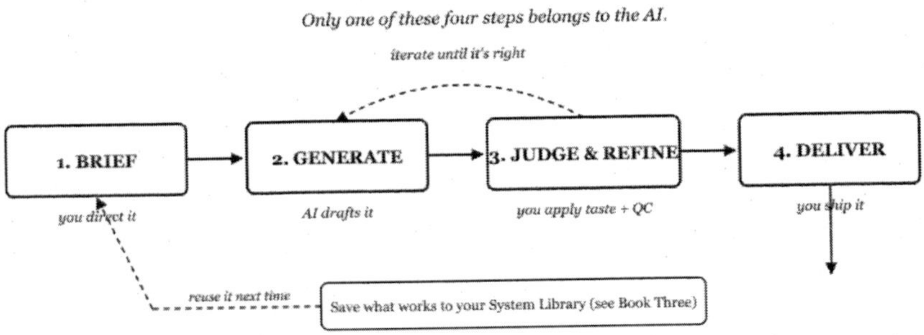

The loop in the figure is the whole operating model on one page. You brief, the AI generates, you judge and refine until it is right, you deliver. Three of those four steps are yours. Only the second belongs to the machine. And the small feedback path matters as much as the loop: every time something works, you save it, so the next job starts from a proven recipe instead of a blank box. That saved library of what works is not a nice-to-have. It is the raw material you will turn into products in Book Three. The operator builds it from day one without thinking of it as building a product, and then one day realizes they already have.

The two traps on the way across

Almost everyone who fails to cross from user to operator fails in one of two specific ways. Name them now so you see them coming.

The first is shipping slop. Generating fast, skipping the judgment step, and sending raw output to a buyer. It feels productive. It is reputation suicide. Speed without quality control is just a faster way to lose clients.

The second is the opposite, and it traps the more careful people. It is endless tinkering. Polishing prompts, testing tools, optimizing a workflow for a client you do not have yet. It feels like work. It produces no income. Refining your craft is only valuable in service of shipping something to someone who can pay. An operator who never delivers is just a user with extra steps.

REALITY CHECK "I just need to perfect my system before I start." No. You perfect the system by starting. The feedback that improves your work comes from real delivery to real buyers, not from another afternoon of prompt tweaking. Ship something rough to one real person this week and you will learn more than a month of solo polishing teaches you.

What the shift actually costs

Honesty, as always. Becoming an operator does not cost money and it does not require talent you lack. It costs a specific discomfort: you have to stop hiding in the chat window and put something with your name on it in front of someone who can reject it. That is the real price. The tool is free or close to it. The courage to deliver is the part you pay.

Everything from here forward assumes you have decided to pay it.

TRY THIS Pull up the list of three skills you wrote at the end of Chapter 1. Pick the one you would feel most confident getting paid for. Now write a full operator brief for one realistic deliverable in that skill, using the seven parts from this chapter: role, audience, goal, the specific point, constraints, format, and quality bar. Run it through ChatGPT. Then do the operator's real job: read the draft as a paying buyer would, and fix the last twenty percent by hand. Keep the brief. You just built the first entry in your System Library, and you are going to use it in Book Two.

You now think like an operator. The next question is where to point all this capability, because pointed at the wrong thing it earns nothing, and pointed at the right thing it compounds. That is the ladder, and it is what the rest of Book One is for. Chapter 3 lays out all three rungs so you can see the whole climb before you take the first step.

Chapter 3
The Skill-to-Income Ladder

You now think like an operator. You can point ChatGPT at a deliverable and produce something worth paying for. Which raises the only question that matters next: pointed at what?

Because here is the trap that swallows capable people. They learn to operate the tool, they feel powerful, and then they spray that power in ten directions at once. A little freelancing here, a half-built course there, an automation they read about on a forum, three abandoned product ideas. Motion everywhere, income nowhere. Capability without a sequence is just expensive busyness.

This chapter gives you the sequence. It is the spine of the entire book, and it is a ladder. Three rungs, climbed in order. Everything in the four books after this one is just a detailed guide to one rung or the move between two of them. Learn the ladder now and you will always know where you are standing and what the next step is.

The Skill-to-Income Ladder

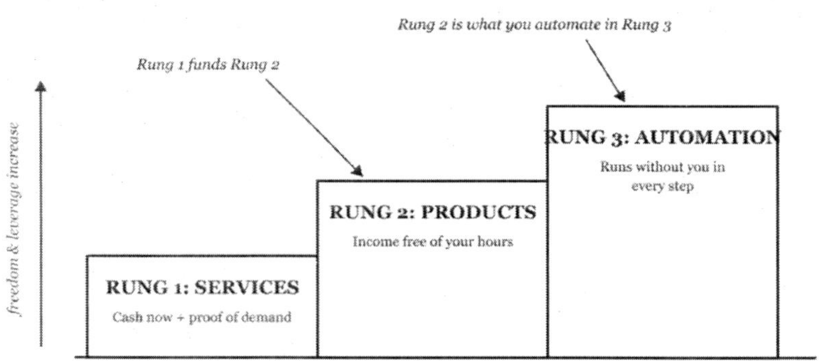

Each rung stands on the one below it.
Skip one and you are building on nothing.

Why a ladder and not a menu

Most books in this field hand you a menu. Here are twelve ways to make money with AI, pick whichever appeals to you. That sounds generous. It is actually how they avoid taking responsibility for your result, because a menu has no order, and order is the entire point.

These three rungs are not options to choose between. They are stages that build on each other. Each one stands on the rung below it, the way the second floor of a house stands on the first. You can no more start at the top than you can build a second floor in mid-air. When you understand why, you will never again be tempted by the "skip straight to passive income" pitch, because you will see it for what it is: an instruction to build on nothing.

> **KEY IDEA** Services, then products, then automation. You earn first, you turn what earns into something that sells without your hours, then you make the whole thing run without you in every step. In that order, because each rung funds and de-risks the next.

Let's walk up it.

Rung 1: Services (earn now)

A service is the most direct way money has ever changed hands. Someone needs a result. You deliver the result. They pay you. With AI, you deliver it faster, at higher quality, and at lower cost than the people who have been charging for it, which is your entire opening.

In practice, a service is a finished thing handed to a buyer. A set of product descriptions for an online store. An edited and proofread manuscript. A month of social posts. A researched market summary. A working landing page. A logo and brand kit. You are not selling "AI services." The buyer does not care what tool you used any more than they care what word processor a writer types in. You are selling the result, and AI is your production team behind the curtain.

What this rung gives you is three things, and the cash is the least important of them. Yes, you get paid this week instead of someday, which matters more than any other feature when you are starting. But you also get something you cannot buy: proof of what people actually pay for. Every time a buyer says yes, the market has told you the truth, with their wallet, about what is valuable. And you get raw material, the briefs and workflows you build to deliver, which become the seed of everything above this rung.

> **PLAIN ENGLISH** Leverage is when your income stops being tied to the hours you put in. With a service, no leverage: stop working and the money stops. The rungs above exist to add leverage. That is what climbing means.

The honest limit of this rung is simple and important: it is capped by your hours and your attention. AI makes each hour far more productive, so your ceiling is much higher than a traditional freelancer's. But it is still a ceiling. There are only so many hours, and a service business, however efficient, eventually runs into them. That ceiling is not a reason to skip this rung. It is the reason the next rung exists.

Rung 2: Products (leverage)

A product is what you get when you take the thing you delivered as a service ten times and package it so it can be sold a hundred times without you doing the work each time. The email sequence you wrote for ten clients becomes a template anyone can buy. The skill you keep getting hired for becomes a course that teaches it. The system you built to organize your own work becomes a downloadable kit.

The magic word here is the one from the box above: leverage. A service trades your hours for money. A product breaks that trade. You do the work once, in the building, and then it earns whether you are working, sleeping, or on a beach. This is the rung where “passive” stops being a lie and becomes a description, because now there is an actual asset doing the earning.

But notice the danger, and notice how the ladder defuses it. A product is a bet on what people want. Build the wrong one and you can pour weeks into something nobody buys. This is exactly where the people who started at rung two, who skipped the climb, lose months and quit. They guessed at demand and guessed wrong.

You will not be guessing. You climbed from rung one, which means you already know what people pay for, because they paid you for it. Your product is not a bet. It is the productized version of a service the market already validated with cash. That single advantage, built into the order of the ladder, is the difference between a product that sells on launch day and a product that sits at zero.

The honest cost of this rung is real: building a good product is concentrated, active work, and the constraint shifts from “can I deliver” to “can I get this in front of enough of the right people.” Marketing and distribution become the new puzzle. That is a better puzzle to have, but it is still a puzzle, and Book Three is where we solve it.

Rung 3: Automation (scale and freedom)

The top rung is where you stop being the person who does each step and become the person who built the machine that does them. You automate the repeatable parts of finding buyers, delivering the work, and running the products, and you stack your streams so they reinforce each other. The business runs largely without you standing in the middle of it.

This is the rung people fantasize about, and it is real. It is also the one that punishes impatience most brutally, because automation does not create a working business. It scales whatever business you already have. Automate something that works and you multiply it. Automate something that does not work yet and you have built a very efficient machine for producing nothing. You cannot automate your way to a business. You automate a business you already built.

The honest cost of this rung is that the systems take effort to build, and you need something proven to point them at. Which is, once again, the entire argument for the ladder: by the time you reach rung three, the lower rungs have handed you a validated service and a selling product. Now you have something worth automating. Book Four and Book Five are this rung.

The progression of freedom

Here is the clearest way to see why you climb. Each rung frees you from something the rung below could not, and reveals the next constraint to solve. That progression is the whole journey on one page.

Rung	Frees you from	But you are still tied to
1. Services	A boss, a salary ceiling, permission to earn	Your own hours, one job at a time
2. Products	Trading hours for money	Getting the product in front of buyers
3. Automation	Doing every step yourself	Maintaining and improving the machine

You never reach a rung with no constraint at all, and anyone who tells you that you will is lying. What you reach is steadily better problems. "I cannot find enough hours" is a worse problem than "I need more traffic," which is a worse problem than "I need to keep the system tuned." You are not climbing toward no work. You are climbing toward work that pays you while you sleep and does not stop when you do.

REALITY CHECK "Why bother with services, I want to build a passive income empire from day one." Because an empire built on a guess is just a pile of unsold products and an abandoned automation. The operators who actually reach the top rung almost all started at the bottom one, and they will tell you the climb was not the slow path. It was the only path that did not waste a year building things nobody wanted. The shortcut is the long way around.

You climb the rungs, you do not abandon them

One correction before we leave the ladder, because the staircase image can mislead. Climbing to rung two does not mean you quit services. Most operators who reach the top run all three rungs at once: services for reliable cash flow and fresh market intelligence, products for leverage, automation tying it together. The ladder describes the order you build in, not a set of doors that close behind you. The services you keep doing are also where you discover your next product. The bottom rung never stops being useful. It just stops being the only thing holding you up.

Where you are right now

You are standing at the foot of the ladder, and that is exactly the right place to be. You have the operator's mindset from Chapter 2 and the map from this chapter. What you do not have yet is the one specific thing to point all of this at, your lane, the intersection of what you can do, what AI makes you fast at, and what people will actually pay for. Choosing it well makes everything above easy and choosing it badly makes everything above a grind. That choice is the last chapter of Book One, and it is next.

TRY THIS Get out your three-skill list from Chapter 1 and the operator brief you wrote in Chapter 2. For each of the three skills, answer one question in a single sentence: what finished result could I sell to a real buyer using this skill and ChatGPT? Not a vague service. A specific deliverable someone could pay for, like "a five-email welcome sequence for online stores" or "a cleaned-up, formatted resume." You are looking for your rung-one entry point. Circle the one that feels both doable this month and genuinely wanted by someone with money. That circled line is where Book Two begins for you.

Chapter 4
Finding Your Lane
(Where Your Skills Meet Real Demand)

At the end of the last chapter I asked you to circle one specific deliverable, your possible entry onto the bottom rung. This chapter decides whether that circle is a lane or a trap, and then turns it into a commitment.

I want to be blunt about why this is the most important decision in the whole book. You can have the operator's mindset, the full ladder, and a hundred hours of effort, and still earn nothing, if you point all of it at the wrong thing. Effort applied to a bad lane is just exhaustion. The same effort applied to the right lane compounds into income. Choosing well is not a step you rush so you can get to the "real" work. Choosing well is the work that makes the rest of the work pay.

So let's choose well.

The three circles

Your lane sits where three things overlap. Miss any one of them and you do not have a business, you have one of three very common disappointments.

Finding Your Lane: The Three-Circle Test

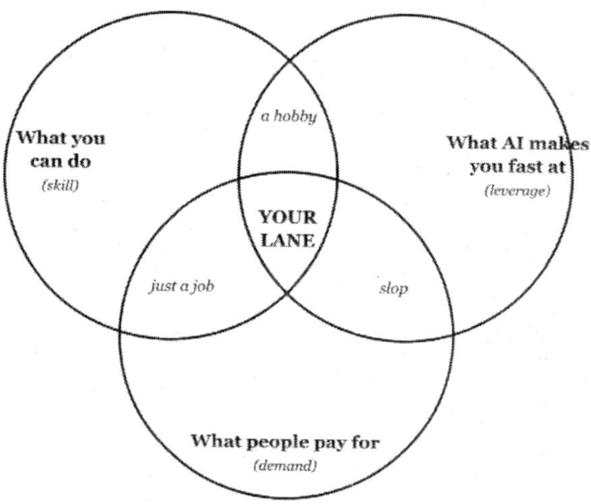

Two circles out of three is a trap with a friendly name. Only the center pays.

The first circle is **what you can do.** Your skill. Not expert-level mastery, just enough competence to deliver a real result and, just as important, enough judgment to tell whether the result is good. This second part matters more than people expect. Remember the operator's loop: you have to judge and refine what the AI produces. If you cannot tell good work from bad in a domain, you cannot do the one job AI cannot do for you. AI raises your floor, so the bar here is lower than it used to be, but it is not zero. You need to be able to recognize quality even where you could not have produced it from scratch.

The second circle is **what AI makes you fast at.** Your leverage. This is where ChatGPT changes the economics, and it is not equally strong everywhere. It is enormously strong on knowledge and language work: writing, editing, research and summarizing, structuring information, drafting code, generating variations, translating, planning. It is weak or useless where the value comes from physical presence, real-time human trust, licensed or regulated expertise, access to proprietary data, or work where a single error is unacceptable. Pick a lane where AI genuinely multiplies you, not one where you will be fighting the tool's limits the whole time.

The third circle is **what people pay for.** Demand. This is the circle beginners ignore, and ignoring it is the single most expensive mistake in this field. Go back to the equation from Chapter 1: AI does nothing for demand. It cannot make people want a thing they do not want. So before you fall in love with an idea, you check, with evidence, that people are already paying for the result, not that they might, not that they should, but that they currently do.

KEY IDEA Your lane is the overlap of all three circles: a result you can deliver and judge, that AI makes you fast at, that people already pay for. All three. Any two without the third is a trap, and each trap has a friendly name that hides what it really is.

The traps with friendly names

The partial overlaps are where most people end up, because each one feels like a business. Look at what they actually are.

You have	But you are missing	What you actually get
Skill + AI leverage	Demand	A hobby. You efficiently produce work nobody is buying. A multiplier on zero demand is still zero.
Skill + Demand	AI leverage	A normal freelance job. Respectable, but you have no edge over every other freelancer and nothing to scale.
AI leverage + Demand	Skill and judgment	Slop. You ship work you cannot even evaluate, the buyer can tell, and your reputation pays the price.

All three	Nothing	Your lane. This is where the money is.

The slop trap deserves a moment, because AI makes it more tempting than ever. It is now possible to produce professional-looking output in a field you know nothing about. People see that and think they have found a shortcut: pick any high-demand skill, let AI do it, collect the money. It does not work, and here is exactly why. You cannot run the judge-and-refine step in a domain where you have no judgment. You will ship the AI's confident mistakes because you cannot see they are mistakes. The buyer, who does have judgment, sees them instantly. This is the path to the angry refund and the one-star review, and it is worth naming so you never take it.

REALITY CHECK "Follow your passion and the money will follow." Often it does not, because passion lives in the first circle and money lives in the third, and they do not always overlap. Plenty of people are passionate about things nobody pays for. Start instead where your competence meets real demand. Here is the part the slogan gets backwards: passion frequently grows out of competence and getting paid, not the other way around. Get good, get paid, and the enthusiasm tends to follow the success.

Narrow beats broad, every time

Here is the instinct I have to talk you out of, because it is the same one that wanted the audience to be "everyone." When you pick your lane, you will feel pressure to keep it wide so you do not turn away business. Resist it. A wide lane is a weak lane.

"AI content services" is not a lane. It is a fog. Nobody wakes up needing "AI content services," and you will be one faceless option among thousands. "Product descriptions for Shopify home-goods stores" is a lane. It is a specific result, for a specific buyer, with a specific problem. That buyer reads it and thinks, that is exactly me. You become the obvious choice instead of a generic option, your outreach gets sharper, your samples get more relevant, and later, when you climb to rung two, you already have a defined audience to sell a product to.

PLAIN ENGLISH A niche is a narrow, specific slice of a market. Not "writing," but "sales emails for dental clinics." Narrow feels smaller and safer to avoid. It is actually the easier path, because in a narrow lane you can become the best and most obvious choice, which you can never be in a wide one.

Narrowing does not shrink your income. It is the thing that gets you your first income at all, because it makes you findable, credible, and specific to a buyer who has a wallet. You can always widen later from a position of strength. You cannot start from everywhere.

Validate before you commit, and do it cheaply

You do not have to bet months to find out if a lane is real. You can de-risk the whole choice in an afternoon, and an afternoon of checking is infinitely cheaper than six months of building the wrong thing.

There are three quick tests, and your candidate lane has to pass all three.

First, **prove the demand is real.** Spend an hour looking for evidence that people currently pay for this exact result. Are freelancers being hired for it right now on the marketplaces? Are businesses spending money on it? Are there existing products selling in this space? You want to see money already moving. Counterintuitively, finding competitors is good news. Competition is proof of demand. An empty market is usually empty for a reason.

Second, **prove you can deliver and judge.** Run the operator's loop once. Using your candidate lane, brief ChatGPT and produce one real sample deliverable, then put on your buyer's eyes and assess it honestly. Could you hand this to a paying client? If you cannot tell, that is your answer: you are missing the skill circle for this lane.

Third, **get one real signal.** Before you go all in, get a single piece of evidence from outside your own head that someone would pay. Show your sample to one person in the target market and ask what they would pay for work like that. Send one quote. Post one offer and see if anyone bites. One genuine signal from a real potential buyer is worth more than a week of your own optimism.

PLAIN ENGLISH Validation just means checking that something is real before you commit to it, using small cheap tests instead of one big expensive bet. In this field it is the difference between the people who earn and the people who spend six months building in the dark.

Commit to one lane, for now

When a candidate passes all three circles and all three tests, do the hard thing: commit to it, and only it, for now.

"For now" is the part that makes this easy. Committing to one lane is not a marriage. It is a starting point. You are choosing where to get your first cash and your first real market feedback, both of which fund and inform everything after. If it turns out to be wrong, you will know fast, because you validated cheaply, and you will pick another with everything you learned. What you cannot do is start in five lanes at once and expect any of them to get the focus it needs to produce income. One lane, run properly, beats five lanes run half-heartedly, every time.

Pick the one. Write it down as a specific sentence: this result, for this buyer. That sentence is your launch point.

The end of Book One

Look at what you are holding now. You understand where money actually comes from and what AI does and does not change about it. You have made the shift from user to operator, the person who directs the tool toward a paying result. You have the full ladder, so you know the whole climb and why its order is not negotiable. And now you have a single, specific, validated lane to point all of it at.

That is the entire foundation. Everything from here is execution, and execution is the fun part, because it is where the money starts. Book Two is rung one: turning your chosen lane into actual income, this month, by landing and delivering your first paying service. It opens by answering the question every honest beginner is secretly asking, which is why we earn with services first instead of chasing the passive dream the title promises. Chapter 5 answers it, and then we go get you paid.

TRY THIS Take your circled candidate and run the full gate on it now, on paper. One: write one sentence each for the three circles, can I do and judge this, does AI make me fast at it, do people already pay for it. Two: spend one hour finding live evidence of demand, real listings, real spend, real competitors. Three: produce one sample deliverable with the operator loop and judge it as a buyer. If it clears all of that, write your commitment sentence, "I deliver [specific result] for [specific buyer]," and put it at the top of a fresh page. That page is your Book Two worksheet. If it does not clear, you just saved yourself months. Pick another candidate and run it again. This afternoon of work is the highest-paid afternoon in the whole book.

Chapter 5

Why Cash Comes Before "Passive"

Let me say out loud the thing you are thinking as Book Two begins.

You bought a book with "millionaire" and "passive income" on the cover, and I am about to spend an entire part of it teaching you to do freelance services. Trading work for money, one job at a time. That is the opposite of passive, and some part of you is wondering whether you have been talked into the slow, boring path while the real money lives somewhere in the back of the book.

I want to answer that suspicion completely, because if I do not, you will rush through this part to get to the "good" chapters, and you will fail there for the exact reason this chapter exists to prevent. So here is the truth: starting with services is not the slow path or the boring path. It is the smartest opening move available to you, and the people who skip it are the ones who never reach the passive income they came for. By the end of this chapter you will want to start here, not tolerate starting here.

Services are a paid education

Here is the reframe that changes everything. Rung one is the only place in this entire business where the market pays you to learn what works.

Think about what products and automation actually require. To build a product that sells, you have to already know what people want and what they will pay. To build automation worth the effort, you have to already have something that works. Both of the higher rungs demand knowledge you do not have yet. There are only two ways to get that knowledge. You can guess, build, and find out the expensive way, which is what the passive-first crowd does and why most of them quit. Or you can let paying clients teach you, in real time, with their own money, exactly what is valuable.

That second path is what a service business is. Every client interaction is a lesson the market is paying you to attend.

> **KEY IDEA** Services are the only rung where you get paid to learn what works. Products and automation require you to already know. Earn first, and the earning teaches you what to build next. That is not a detour on the way to passive income. It is how you find out which passive income to build.

What the lessons actually are

A service business teaches you four things you cannot learn any other way, and you will need all four above this rung.

You learn **what people actually pay for**, not what you assumed they would. The first time a client happily pays for something you thought was trivial, or shrugs at something you thought was your best work, the market has corrected your instincts for free.

You learn **what they will pay**, which is information no blog post can give you, because it depends on your specific lane, your buyers, and the results you deliver.

You learn **what is repeatable.** When you find yourself delivering the same thing for the fifth client, you have just discovered a product. You did not brainstorm it. The work handed it to you.

And you learn **what is tedious.** The parts of delivery you dread doing again are the exact parts you will automate later. You do not have to guess what to systematize. Your own groaning tells you.

Notice what is happening. The two rungs above this one are made of these four lessons, and services hand them to you while paying you to receive them. That is why we climb in this order. Not because services are humble beginnings, but because services are reconnaissance you get paid for.

Forget what you knew about freelancing

The old objection to services was fair, once. Freelancing meant trading hours for money with a hard ceiling, a job without a boss, no leverage, no scale. For decades that was true, and it is why "passive income" became the dream in the first place: it was the escape from the time-for-money trap.

AI broke that trap, and most people have not updated their thinking yet. When each hour of your work now produces what used to take three or four, the economics of a service business change completely. You can deliver faster than the people you compete with, charge for the result rather than the hour, take on more without drowning, and raise your effective rate as you get sharper. The ceiling is still there, but it is now far higher, and you reach the point where it is worth climbing past long before it constrains you.

So the service business you are about to build is not your grandfather's freelancing. It is the most efficient first business a single person has ever been able to start, and it happens to also be a paid education in what to build next. There has not been a better opening move in a long time.

The three returns of a single service

When you complete one piece of paid work, you do not get one thing. You get three, and only one of them is the money.

What you earn	What it is	What it funds on the climb

Cash	Money in hand this week	The time and tools to build products without going broke first
Knowledge	Proof of what sells, at what price, to whom	The de-risking of every product you build above this rung
Relationships	Buyers who now know and trust you	Your first product customers, who are far easier to sell to than strangers

This is why services compound and why skipping them is so costly. The passive-first builder, alone in a room betting on a guess, gets none of these three until and unless the guess pays off. The services-first builder banks all three with every job, and each return makes the next rung easier and safer. You are not just earning. You are buying down the risk of everything that comes after.

The valley most people quit in

Now the argument that matters most, because it is about whether you stay in the game long enough to win it.

When Does the Money Actually Start?

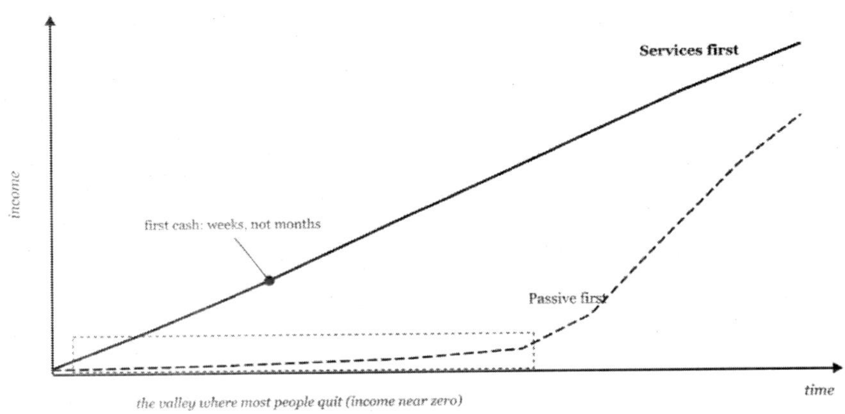

Illustrative shape, not a forecast. The point is when income starts, not how much.

Look at the two paths. The passive-first path has a long flat stretch at the start where income sits near zero. You build, you launch, you wait, and for a stretch that feels much longer than it is, nothing comes back. That flat stretch is a valley, and it is where the overwhelming majority of people quit. Not because the strategy was wrong in theory, but because human motivation cannot survive an unbroken run of effort with no reward. They run out of belief before they run out of road.

The services-first path does not have that valley. Income starts early, in weeks rather than months, because you are delivering real work to real buyers from the start. That early cash is worth far more than its dollar value, because it is proof. It tells your brain this is real, this works, keep going. Momentum is not a soft, motivational nicety. It is the hard asset that keeps you climbing when the passive-first builder has already given up.

PLAIN ENGLISH Runway is how long you can keep going before you run out of money or belief, whichever comes first. The passive-first path burns both during its long zero-income valley. The services-first path refills both from week one. Longer runway is how you survive long enough to reach the leverage.

REALITY CHECK "But passive income is the whole point, why delay it." You are not delaying it. You are funding it, de-risking it, and surviving long enough to build it. The passive income you came for is real and it is coming, in Book Three. Services are not the thing standing between you and it. Services are the thing that gets you there with money in the bank, proof of what to build, and customers waiting. Skip them and you arrive at the product rung broke, guessing, and alone, which is to say you do not arrive at all.

An honest word on timeline

I will not print numbers, because anyone who promises you a specific figure by a specific date is lying, and you would be right to distrust them. But I will be honest about shape, because shape you can plan around.

With a validated lane from Chapter 4, your first paid service is realistically a matter of weeks of focused effort, not months. It will be modest. First income usually is. Products, by contrast, often earn nothing for a real stretch while you build and find your audience, and some never earn at all. Put those two facts together and the conclusion is unavoidable: services are not only the safest first money, they are the fastest money, period. The path that feels like the shortcut to riches is actually the slowest route to your first dollar, and the "slow" path pays you first.

That is the entire case. Earn first because it teaches you, funds you, de-risks you, and keeps you in the game. Everything above this rung is built out of what you learn and bank down here.

What's next

You are committed to earning first, and you have a validated lane from Book One. The next question is purely practical: what exactly do you sell, how do you package it so a buyer says yes, and how do you price the result instead of your hours. That is your offer, and a sharp offer is the difference between a lane and an income. Chapter 6 builds it.

TRY THIS Open your Book Two worksheet, the page with your commitment sentence on it. Underneath it, write one date: the day you intend to send your first real offer to a real potential buyer. Make it close, within two to three weeks. Then write a single line reframing the higher rungs, in your own words, something like: "Products and automation come later, and this service is what funds and teaches them." Read that line whenever you feel the pull to skip ahead. Your job for the rest of Book Two is to hit that date with something worth paying for, and the next chapter builds exactly that.

Chapter 6
Building an Offer People Actually Pay For

You have a lane and a date on the calendar. Now you need the thing you put in front of a buyer when that date arrives, and it is not "I do AI services." It is an offer, and the difference between a lane and an offer is the difference between knowing what field you are in and having something a person can actually hand you money for.

This is a hands-on chapter. By the end of it you will have a written offer, drafted with help, stress-tested, and sharpened to a single sentence, ready to send.

A lane is a direction. An offer is a thing you can buy.

Most beginners stop at the lane and wonder why no money arrives. They say "I write marketing copy with AI" and expect buyers to fill in the rest. But "I write marketing copy" is not something you can purchase. It is a category, and nobody buys a category. They buy a specific result, for a specific need, at a known price, with a clear idea of what they are getting.

An offer turns your lane into exactly that: a packaged, specific, buyable thing. A clear offer to a narrow buyer outsells a vague offer to everyone, every time.

The six parts of an offer

Every offer that sells has the same six parts. Get all six right and selling becomes easy, because the offer does most of the persuading for you.

Anatomy of an Offer People Can Actually Buy

THE RESULT	*A welcome sequence that turns subscribers into buyers*	the outcome, not the task
WHO IT'S FOR	*Shopify stores selling home goods*	narrow, not everyone
YOU GET	*5 ready-to-paste emails + subject lines*	concrete, handed over
SCOPE	*2 revision rounds. Copy only, not setup.*	boundaries protect your time
PRICE	*One flat project price*	priced on the result, never the hour
PROOF	*A free sample email, judge before you buy*	removes the buyer's risk

Six parts. Miss the price logic or the scope and the offer leaks money.

The result. What the buyer gets, stated as an outcome, not a task. Not "I will write you five emails," which is a task, but "a welcome sequence that turns new subscribers into first-time buyers," which is a result. Buyers do not want emails. They want more sales. Lead with what they actually want.

The buyer. Who it is for, narrow, straight from your lane. Naming the buyer specifically is not exclusion, it is a magnet.

The deliverable. The concrete thing that changes hands, described so plainly there is no confusion.

The scope. What is included and, just as important, what is not. This single part saves you from the most common way service providers lose money: the project that never ends.

The price. How much, framed around the result. We spend real time on this below.

The proof. The reason to believe you can deliver, and the thing that removes the buyer's fear. A free sample, a relevant example, a simple guarantee.

Drafting your offer

You do not have to write it from a blank page. Hand ChatGPT your lane and let it produce a first draft of all six parts, then you do the operator's work of sharpening it.

> PROMPT — Draft your offer from your lane "You are helping me turn a service lane into a clear, buyable offer. My lane is: [your lane, for example 'welcome email sequences for Shopify home-goods stores']. Draft an offer with these six parts, each in one or two lines: (1) the result, stated as an outcome the buyer wants, not a task; (2) the specific buyer; (3) the concrete deliverable they receive; (4) the scope, including what is NOT included; (5) the pricing logic, and do not invent a number, just describe what I should anchor the price on; (6) a proof or risk-remover I could offer. Be specific and concrete. No hype words."

The shape of this prompt is the lesson, not the exact wording. You give it your lane, you force a fixed six-part structure so it cannot wander, and you ban hype, which is AI's default register. Swap the bracketed lane for yours and it works in any field, today or after the next model update, because it is a structure, not a magic phrase. What comes back is a starting point. The sharpening is yours.

The one principle that changes your income: sell the result, not the hour

Here is the most important idea in this chapter, and it runs against instinct.

AI makes you fast. Work that once took a skilled person two days might now take you two hours. The instinct is to price by time, so you charge for two hours. Do that and you have handed the entire benefit of AI to your buyer and kept none of it. Worse, you have built a business that punishes efficiency: the faster you work, the less you earn.

You price on the result, because that is what the buyer values. A welcome sequence that lifts a store's sales is worth the same to that store whether you spent two days or two hours. The buyer is not paying for your time. They are paying for the outcome. AI is your private advantage, the reason you deliver that outcome faster and at better margins than competitors. Pricing by the hour throws the advantage away.

> KEY IDEA Never price by your time, and especially never by your AI-shortened time. Price on the result the buyer is buying. Your speed is your margin, not your discount.

Pricing honestly, without racing to the bottom

I will not print prices, because the right number depends on your lane, your buyer, and the moment, and the companion resource keeps live ranges. But the thinking is durable. Anchor on three things: the value of the result to the buyer, the market rate you learned during your Chapter 4 research, and your floor, the price below which the work is not worth your effort, which is emphatically not your AI-reduced cost. Then refuse the move that feels safest and is actually fatal.

> REALITY CHECK "I'll win business by being cheaper, since AI makes my costs low." Everyone's costs are low now. AI handed the whole market the same discount, so "cheap" is no longer an edge, it is a floor a million people stand on. Compete there and you win a race whose prize is exhaustion. Compete instead on the result, the specificity, the reliability, and the absence of hassle. Buyers pay more, gladly, for the person who clearly understands their exact problem and removes the risk.

It is fine to start at a modest price to land your first one or two clients and collect proof. Treat that as a deliberate, temporary move to buy credibility, then raise it once you have a testimonial. Starting low to start is strategy. Staying low is a trap.

> PLAIN ENGLISH A productized service is a service packaged like a product: fixed scope, fixed deliverable, fixed price. Instead of "hire me by the hour for whatever," it is "this exact thing, for this exact price." It is easier to sell, easier to deliver, and it is the first step toward the products you build in Book Three.

Write it down

An offer in your head is not an offer. Fill in this structure, in language your buyer would use about themselves.

TEMPLATE — The offer one-pager THE RESULT: [the outcome the buyer wants] WHO IT'S FOR: [the specific buyer] YOU GET: [the concrete deliverable] SCOPE: [what is included]. Not included: [the boundaries] PRICE: [one flat project price, anchored on the result and the market, with a floor that is not your AI cost] PROOF: [the sample or guarantee that removes the buyer's risk]

One-sentence version: "I help [specific buyer] get [specific result] with [specific deliverable]."

The one-sentence version is the part you will use constantly, in messages, in conversations, in your own head. If you can say it and have a real buyer nod, you have an offer. If they look confused, keep sharpening.

Stress-test it before you send it

Before that offer goes anywhere, turn ChatGPT into the skeptic you are afraid of meeting, and let it find the holes while it is free to do so.

PROMPT — Stress-test your offer "Here is my offer: [paste the six parts]. Act as a skeptical buyer in my target market who has been burned before. Tell me, bluntly: (1) where it sounds generic or could apply to anyone; (2) where it sells a task instead of a result; (3) what would make me hesitate or distrust it; (4) where the scope is loose enough to cause a problem later. Then rewrite the single weakest line to be sharper. Do not be encouraging."

The "do not be encouraging" line matters, because AI's instinct is to praise you, and praise teaches you nothing. Forcing it into the role of a burned, skeptical buyer turns it into a free editor for the exact weaknesses that lose sales.

The offer mistakes that quietly kill the sale

Check your draft against these before you send it.

The mistake	Why it kills the sale	The fix
Vague offer ("I do AI content")	Nobody can buy a category, only a specific thing	Name one result for one buyer
Selling the task, not the result	Tasks feel like a commodity and invite haggling	Lead with the outcome the buyer wants
Pricing by the hour	Caps your income and punishes efficiency	Price on the result, keep speed as margin
Competing on cheapest	Everyone is cheap now, so it is no edge	Compete on specificity and risk removal
No scope boundaries	The project never ends and your margin bleeds	State what is and is not included, up front

No proof or sample	The buyer fears wasting money and stalls	Offer a sample or guarantee to remove risk

A full worked example

Watch a real offer go from unbuyable to sharp. Here is what a beginner in our running lane typically writes first:

“I offer AI-powered email marketing services for businesses. I can write emails, newsletters, and campaigns to help grow your sales. Affordable rates, fast turn-around.”

Run that through the stress-test prompt and the verdict is brutal, and correct. It is a category, not a thing. The buyer is “businesses,” which means no one. It sells tasks, writing emails, not a result. It has no scope, so the first client will ask for ten rounds of free revisions. It competes on “affordable,” the race to the bottom. And it offers no proof. Nobody can buy this, because there is nothing specific to buy.

Now the same lane, built through the six parts:

THE RESULT: turn new subscribers into first-time buyers WHO IT’S FOR: Shopify stores selling home goods YOU GET: a five-email welcome sequence, written and ready to paste in, with subject lines SCOPE: two rounds of revisions, copy only, not technical setup PRICE: one flat project price, anchored on the sales a working sequence brings in, not on my hours PROOF: a free sample of the opening email, so you judge the quality before paying

One-sentence version: “I help Shopify home-goods stores turn new subscribers into first-time buyers with a five-email welcome sequence.”

Same skill, same person, same lane. The first version gets ignored and the second gets bought, and every fix traces back to one of the six parts. That is the whole job of this chapter: not writing more, but being specific enough that a real person can say yes.

What’s next

You have something to sell. The next question is who to sell it to, and how to reach them with no audience, network, or following. A perfect offer that nobody sees earns nothing. Chapter 7 is how you find your first clients from a standing start, with the prompts and templates to do it.

TRY THIS Build your offer now, on your Book Two worksheet. Use the draft prompt to generate a first version of the six parts from your lane. Fill in the offer one-pager template in your own words, fixing what the draft got generic. Then run the stress-test prompt and let the skeptical-buyer version tear into it, and rewrite the weakest line. Finish by writing the one-sentence version and saying it aloud. If it does not sound like something a specific person would buy, keep cutting until it does. Save the final offer and both prompts to your System Library. This is what you put in front of the clients you find next.

Chapter 7
Finding Clients When Nobody Knows Your Name

This is the chapter people skip to and the chapter people fear. You have an offer now, a real one, six parts, sharpened to a sentence. The terror is the next step: putting it in front of strangers who have never heard of you, with no audience, no reputation, and no following to lean on.

I am not going to pretend that fear away. I am going to dismantle the thing causing it and then hand you the exact prompts, templates, and a full worked example so you are never staring at a blank message wondering what to type. By the end of this chapter you will have sent something.

You do not need an audience

The wrong picture goes like this: first I build a following, then I become known, then clients come to me. It sounds responsible. It is the single slowest path to your first dollar, and it dumps you straight into the valley from Chapter 5, months of posting into the void with no income and no proof that any of it works.

Here is the right picture. You do not need many people to know you. You need to reach the few right people directly and make them a clear, low-risk offer. Your first clients will not come from an audience. They will come from you reaching out, on purpose, to specific people who have the exact problem your offer solves.

> **KEY IDEA** You do not need the many to know you. You need to reach the right few directly. First clients come from targeted outreach and warm proximity, not from building a following. Direct beats famous, every single time you are starting out.

Where the work actually is

There are four places your first clients come from, and they differ along two lines that matter: how warm the buyer is, meaning how ready they are to trust and pay you, and how many of them you can reach.

Where Your First Clients Actually Come From

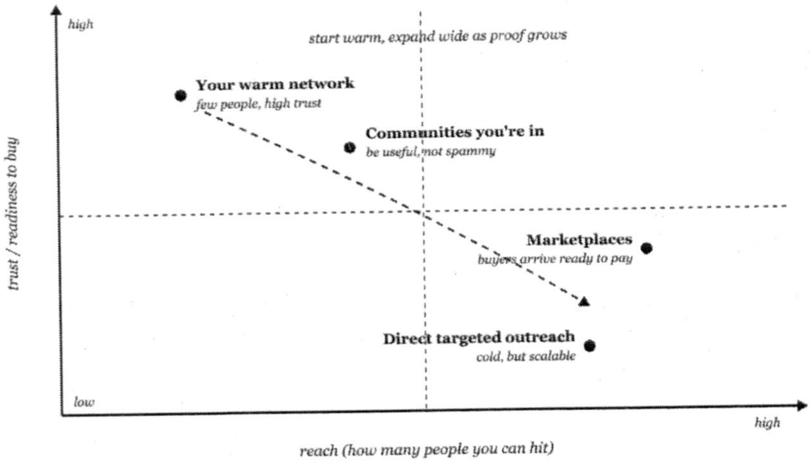

No audience required. You need to reach the right few directly, not the many vaguely.

Your warm network is people who already know you, even slightly. Few in number, but the trust is already there, which makes them the easiest first yes you will ever get. **Communities where your buyers gather** are the forums and groups where your lane already hangs out; you win there by being useful, not by dropping flyers. **Direct targeted outreach** is reaching specific people who visibly have your problem, cold; low trust to start, but high reach, and it is the workhorse channel. **Freelance marketplaces** are the one channel where buyers arrive already wanting to pay, which often makes them the fastest route to a first paid piece of proof.

The strategy the diagram encodes is simple: start warm to get your first one or two clients and your first proof, then expand toward the high-reach channels as that proof accumulates.

Now the practical part, channel by channel, with the words to actually use.

Reaching your warm network

The mistake here is treating it like a sales pitch to a stranger. It is not. It is a low-key heads-up to someone who already trusts you. The tone is casual, the ask is soft, and you give them an easy way to say "not me, but I know someone."

TEMPLATE — The warm-network message Hey [name], quick one. I've started helping [buyer type] [result] using [deliverable]. You came to mind, partly because [specific reason, or: I figured you might know the right person]. No pressure at all, just wanted to put it on your radar in case it's useful to you or someone you know.

Keep it short, keep it human, and genuinely mean the "no pressure." The goal of a warm message is not always to land that person. It is often to get pointed at the person behind them.

Reaching out directly (the workhorse)

Cold outreach scares people because they picture writing a hundred messages from scratch. You will not. You will research fast, draft with AI, and add the human touch that makes it land. Here is the exact sequence.

Step one is research, because a message that proves you actually looked at their business beats a generic pitch every time. ChatGPT turns twenty minutes of research into two.

PROMPT — Research a prospect "You are helping me prepare a short, specific outreach message. Here is information about a business: [paste their website text, About page, or a description]. In five bullet points, tell me: (1) what they sell, (2) who their customer is, (3) one likely problem they have related to [your lane], (4) one specific, genuine detail about them I could reference to prove I actually looked, and (5) the single result they would care about most. Be concrete and skip the flattery."

Notice why this prompt is built the way it is, because the pattern matters more than the exact words. You give it the raw material, you ask for a fixed, numbered output so it cannot ramble, and you explicitly forbid flattery, which is AI's default filler. You can adapt this for any lane by swapping the bracketed parts. It does not depend on which model you use, today's or next year's, because it is a thinking structure, not a magic phrase.

Step two is the draft. Hand the research straight back to it.

PROMPT — Draft a tailored message "Here is a prospect: [paste the five research bullets]. Here is my offer: [paste your one-sentence offer]. Draft a short outreach message, under 90 words, that opens with the specific detail about them, names the problem, states the result I deliver, offers a free [sample / mini-audit], and ends with one easy question. Plain and human, no hype, no flattery. Give me two versions with different openers."

Step three, the one that separates you from the spammers, is yours and yours alone: you read both drafts as the buyer would, pick the stronger opener, and replace anything that sounds like a robot with the specific, true detail from your research. That is the operator's judge-and-refine step from Chapter 2, applied to outreach. We will watch it happen in the worked example below.

Here is the structure your final message should always have, whoever drafted it.

> **TEMPLATE — The direct first-contact message** Hi [name], [Specific detail from your research that proves you looked at their business.] A lot of [their type of business] run into [specific problem]. I help [buyer] get [result] by [deliverable]. I went ahead and made a quick [free sample / mini-audit] for you, no strings: [link]. Worth a look? [your name]

Reaching buyers on marketplaces

Marketplace buyers have already raised their hand. Your job is not to convince them they have a problem, it is to stand out from the other applicants, and you do that with specificity, never with the lowest price.

> **PROMPT — Tailor a marketplace proposal** "Here is a job posting: [paste it]. Here is my offer: [paste your one-sentence offer]. Write a short proposal, under 120 words, that shows in the first line that I understood their specific need, states the exact result and deliverable, mentions one relevant proof point or sample I can show, and ends with a clear next step. Do not restate the job back to them, and cut all generic filler."

The "do not restate the job back to them" instruction is doing real work, because that restating is exactly what generic AI proposals do, and exactly what buyers skim past. Forbidding it forces the draft to be about value, not summary.

The message that gets a reply

Across all four channels, the difference between deleted and answered is the same.

The message that gets ignored	The message that gets a reply
Opens about you ("I'm a freelancer offering...")	Opens about them, showing you actually looked
Generic, clearly sent to hundreds	Specific to their business and their problem
Sells your services	Leads with the result they want
Asks for a big commitment ("hire me")	Asks for something small and low-risk
Long, all about your skills	Short, all about their outcome

No proof, just claims	Includes or offers a sample they can judge

Read the right column as one idea: make it about them, lead with the result, keep it short, and make saying yes nearly free.

Use AI to tailor, never to spam

REALITY CHECK "AI lets me send a thousand outreach messages a day." It does, and that is the trap, not the opportunity. Every inbox on earth is drowning in obvious AI spam, and people delete it on sight. Mass-blasting generic messages does not scale your results, it scales your rejection, and on many platforms it gets you flagged or banned. The edge in an age of infinite spam is the opposite of spam: personalization, which is exactly what the prompts above are built to help you do well. Ten genuinely tailored messages beat a thousand generic ones, and it is not close.

A full worked example

Let me run one real prospect through the whole sequence so you see the judgment, not just the prompts. Say your offer is: "I help Shopify home-goods stores turn new subscribers into first-time buyers with a five-email welcome sequence."

You find a small store, Maple & Stone, selling handmade ceramic homeware. You paste their site into the research prompt, and it gives you back something like this:

- Sells handmade ceramic mugs, bowls, and vases, mid-to-premium price.
- Customers are design-conscious adults furnishing their homes, plus gift buyers.
- Likely problem: they capture emails with a discount popup but probably send little afterward, so new subscribers go cold.
- Specific detail: the popup offers ten percent off, but there is no visible welcome email following it up, and their About page leads hard with the maker's story.
- The result they would care about most: turning a discount signup into an actual first purchase.

You feed that into the draft prompt. The first version it hands back is weak, and it is worth seeing exactly how weak, because this is what most people would copy and send:

"Hi, I'm a freelance email marketer specializing in AI-powered email campaigns. I help businesses like yours boost sales with high-converting email sequences.

I'd love to work with you. Are you available for a quick call this week?"

Look at everything wrong with it. It opens about the sender. It is generic enough to send to any business on earth. It sells the service, not the result. It asks for a big commitment, a call, from someone who has never heard of you. And it offers no proof. That is slop, and it would be ignored.

Now you do the operator's job. You take the structure, you drop the specific research detail in, you lead with the result, you shrink the ask, and you add proof:

"Hi [name], I love that Maple & Stone leads with the maker's story, that's the kind of thing that makes people actually want to buy. I noticed you offer ten percent off to new subscribers, but it doesn't look like there's a welcome email picking up where the popup leaves off, and that gap is usually where the first sale is won or lost. I help home-goods stores turn new subscribers into first-time buyers with a short welcome sequence. I drafted the opening email for Maple & Stone so you can see the quality first, no strings: [link]. Want me to send it over?"

Same offer, same tool, same two minutes of research. One version gets deleted and one gets a reply, and the only difference is the operator's judgment in the final pass. That pass is the job. The AI got you ninety percent of the way in seconds. The last ten percent, the part that actually lands the client, is yours.

Remove the risk and the first yes comes

When you have no reputation, the buyer's biggest objection is unspoken: what if I pay this stranger and get garbage. Answer it before they raise it. The most powerful tool you have for your first few clients is to make their risk close to zero with a free sample, a small no-obligation piece, a quick audit, exactly the "no strings" sample in the templates above. With no track record, proof beats promises, because they are no longer trusting your word, they are trusting their own eyes. Treat this as deliberate, temporary scaffolding to earn your first one to three proof clients and their testimonials, then stop, because now you have proof and proof lets you charge full price.

Follow up, because most replies come on the second touch

Most people send one message, hear nothing, and quit on that prospect. A single, light follow-up a few days later recovers a surprising number of them, because the first message simply got buried, not rejected.

PROMPT — Write a follow-up "Write a one-line, friendly follow-up to this message I sent a few days ago with no reply: [paste it]. Assume they are busy, not uninterested. Add one small new piece of value or make the ask even lighter. Keep it under 30 words, no guilt-tripping."

One follow-up is helpful. Five is harassment. Send one, then move on.

The honest truth about volume

Outreach is a numbers game, but a targeted one, and you must make peace with one fact: most people will not respond. That is not failure, that is the job working as designed. The ones who succeed are not the ones who get a yes every time. They are the ones who send enough good, tailored attempts that the noes stop stinging and the occasional yes lands. Do not read early silence as a verdict on you. Read it as the cost of doing business, and keep sending quality attempts consistently.

The first yes changes everything

Landing your first client is the hardest single step in this book, and once you take it, the slope tilts in your favor for good. That first client gives you a testimonial, which warms every cold channel. They give you a referral, often your easiest second client. And they give you the lived proof that this works. From there it compounds.

What's next

Getting the yes is only half of rung one. The other half is delivering so well that the client comes back, refers you, and lets you raise your price, while never shipping the kind of raw output that quietly destroys a reputation. Chapter 8 makes sure you do not.

TRY THIS Build your prospect list: at least ten specific targets across the channels in the diagram. Then actually run the sequence on your first three. For the cold ones, use the research prompt, then the draft prompt, then do the operator's final pass yourself, just like the worked example, dropping in the real detail and shrinking the ask. For anyone warm, use the warm-network template. Send all three before the date you set in Chapter 5, and save the prompts and your edited messages to your System Library so the next round takes minutes. The goal of this chapter is not a perfect message. It is three sent ones.

Chapter 8
Delivering at Speed Without Wrecking Your Reputation

A first client says yes. This is the moment Book Two has been driving toward, and it is also the moment a surprising number of beginners quietly throw it all away. They win the client, they get excited, and then they fumble the delivery, and the client who was about to become a testimonial, a referral, and repeat income becomes a refund and a warning to others instead.

Delivery is not the boring part after the sale. Delivery is your reputation, made one job at a time. This chapter is about doing it fast, because AI lets you, without ever shipping the kind of work that ends a reputation before it starts. It comes with the exact checks, prompts, and messages to do that.

The two ways to ruin a delivery

There are exactly two ways to wreck this, and they are opposites, which is why people fall into one while running from the other.

The first is shipping too fast. You let AI produce the work, you give it a glance, and you send it. The client opens it and immediately sees what it is: generic, possibly wrong, clearly not made for them. That is slop, and it loses you the client, their referrals, and their repeat business.

The second is over-polishing. Terrified of imperfection, you fuss for so long that the entire speed advantage AI gave you evaporates. You protected your reputation and destroyed your margin.

The operator walks the line.

How you deliver	What happens	The result
Fast and sloppy	Client sees raw, generic, or wrong work	Refund, bad review, no referrals
Slow and over-polished	Good work, but the speed advantage is gone	Exhaustion, no margin, cannot scale
Operator: fast to the gate, judged through it	Delivered quickly and worth the buyer's trust	Testimonial, referral, repeat, a raise

The delivery quality gate

Everything you deliver passes through the same checkpoint before it reaches a client. AI gets you there fast. The checkpoint is all judgment, and nothing ships until it passes.

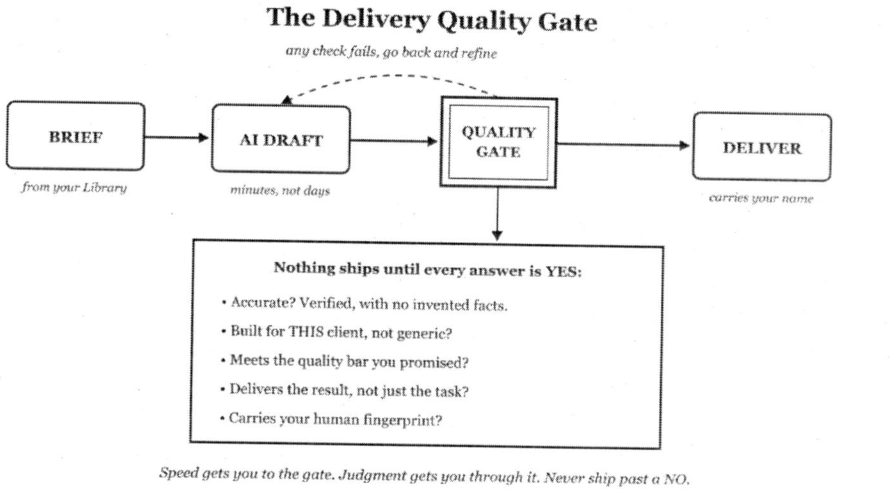

This is the operator's loop from Chapter 2 applied to paid work, with the judgment step turned into a hard gate. Make it literal by keeping this checklist where you work.

TEMPLATE — The delivery gate checklist Before this leaves my hands, every answer must be YES: [ ] Accurate? Every checkable claim verified, no invented facts. [ ] Built for THIS client, not generic? [ ] Meets the quality bar I promised in the offer? [ ] Delivers the result, not just the task? [ ] Carries my human fingerprint? Any NO sends it back. No exceptions, no "close enough."

Two of those checks are where AI-assisted work most often fails, so they get prompts of their own.

The accuracy check, and why AI cannot do it for you

AI invents facts, numbers, names, and sources with total confidence. This is the single most dangerous thing about delivering AI-assisted work, because the errors do not look like errors.

PLAIN ENGLISH A hallucination is when AI states something false as if it were certainly true. It is not lying, it has no idea it is wrong, which is what makes it dangerous. A confident, fluent, fabricated fact reads exactly like a real one.

You can use AI to help you find what needs checking, but never to confirm that its own output is correct, because it cannot. The honest use is to make it surface every claim, then you verify them yourself.

PROMPT — Surface what to verify "Here is a draft I am about to deliver: [paste]. List every factual claim in it that a reader could check: statistics, percentages, names, dates, prices, product features, and any 'studies show' statements. Present them as a checklist. Do NOT tell me whether they are correct, because you cannot verify your own output. Just surface everything I must confirm myself before this ships."

The instruction telling it not to vouch for its own accuracy is not a formality. It is the whole point. The prompt's job is to build you a verification to-do list, not to give you false confidence.

The "for this client" check

Generic output is the unmistakable signature of slop. The fix is to inject the specific.

PROMPT — Make it for this client "Here is a draft and details about the specific client it is for. Draft: [paste]. Client context: [paste who they are, their voice, the specific details of their situation]. Rewrite the draft so it is unmistakably for THIS client: use their context, match their voice, and replace anything generic that could apply to any client with something specific to them. Then flag any line that still feels generic after your pass."

If you could send the exact same deliverable to any other client in your lane, it is not ready.

A worked example: catching what would have wrecked you

Say you are delivering the opening welcome email for our home-goods store, Maple & Stone. AI drafts it fast, and buried in the draft is this line:

"Studies show welcome emails generate 320% more revenue than regular promotional emails, so you're already ahead just by reading this."

It sounds authoritative. It is also exactly the kind of thing you must never ship. You run the surface-what-to-verify prompt, and it flags the "320%" and the "studies show" as claims you cannot confirm. You go looking, and you cannot find a credible, current source for that exact figure. So you do not ship it. You cut the fake precision and rewrite to something true and defensible: that welcome emails reliably outperform generic blasts because they reach people at their most interested. Same persuasive point, no fabricated statistic with your name under it.

Then you notice the draft's opening line is generic: *"Welcome to our store! We're so glad you're here."* That could be any store on earth. You run the make-it-for-this-client prompt with Maple & Stone's context, and it becomes something only they could send, leading with the maker and the craft that their own About page leads with. One pass caught a hallucination that would have embarrassed you in front of a client, and one pass turned anonymous filler into something specific. That is the gate doing its job.

Speed without slop

The gate protects quality. Here is how you keep speed. Reuse your System Library, so each job starts from a proven recipe, not a blank box. Front-load the brief, because ten minutes of precise briefing saves an hour of fixing. And match your effort to the result, not to your perfectionism: deliver work that delights the buyer, then stop, because polishing past the point the client notices only burns your margin.

> **KEY IDEA** Speed gets you to the gate. Judgment gets you through it. The gate is the one place you never rush, because it is the only thing standing between fast delivery and a wrecked reputation. Never ship past a NO.

Do you tell them you use AI?

> **REALITY CHECK** "Isn't it dishonest to use AI and not say so?" No. Clients buy a result, not a method, the same way they never asked which software a designer uses. You are not obligated to advertise your tools. You are absolutely obligated to stand behind the result as your own. The line is not "did AI touch this," it is "can I personally vouch for this as my work and my judgment." If you ran it through the gate, verified it, made it specific, and put your fingerprint on it, it is your work, produced with a tool. If you could not vouch for it, the problem was never the AI. It was that you skipped the gate.

So do not hide, and do not advertise. Own the quality.

Manage the client, and start the flywheel

The deliverable is most of the job, not all of it. Set expectations up front and hold the scope from your offer, so revisions do not become a free buffet. Deliver when you said you would, because reliability is rarer than talent. And when you hand the work over, do the two small things that start everything compounding.

TEMPLATE — Delivery message that earns the testimonial and referral
Hi [name], here is [deliverable]. [One line on how it delivers the result and how to put it to use.] I kept it to [scope reminder, if useful]. If it is useful, two quick things whenever you have a moment: a sentence I could use as a testimonial, and whether you know one other [buyer type] who has the same need. Either way, glad to have done this for you. [your name]

A single well-delivered job hands you a testimonial that warms every cold channel, a referral that is your easiest next client, repeat work that costs nothing to win, and the proof that lets you raise your price. One good delivery spins all four at once. That flywheel is rung one working as designed, and it runs on delivering well, every time.

The end of Book Two

Stand back. You can choose a lane, build an offer, find clients from a standing start, and deliver work that earns trust, repeat business, and referrals. That is a complete service business, the bottom rung, and the cash, proof, and relationships it generates fund everything above it. You have also been building your System Library with every delivery, and that library is the raw material for the next rung, because the moment you have delivered the same thing for the fifth time, the market has handed you a validated product. That is where Book Three begins. Chapter 9 shows you the product hiding inside the service you already deliver.

> **TRY THIS** Turn the gate checklist into a literal document at the top of your delivery workspace. Before your first client work ships, run the surface-what-to-verify prompt and confirm every flagged claim yourself, then run the make-it-for-this-client prompt with your client's real details. Do not let anything past a single NO. When you deliver, use the delivery message template to hand it over and ask for the testimonial and referral. Then save the prompts, the checklist, and the workflow to your System Library. You just delivered a service and, without slowing down, gathered the first ingredient for a product.

Chapter 9
Turning a Service Into a Product

Welcome to the rung you came for. Book Three is leverage, the place where your income finally stops being chained to your hours, and where the word on your cover, passive, becomes an honest description instead of a fantasy. You earned your way here the right way, with a working service business beneath you, and that changes everything about how this rung will go for you compared to the people who tried to start here.

Because here is the thing those people never understood, and it is the whole secret of this chapter: you are not going to invent a product. You are going to find one you already have.

The product is hiding in the work you already do

At the end of the last chapter I pointed at a signal: the fifth time you deliver the same thing. That repetition is not boredom. It is the market showing you a product, in broad daylight, paid for in advance.

Think about what your service business has been quietly doing. Every delivery, you saved a brief and a workflow to your System Library. Every client taught you what they would pay for and what they valued. After a handful of similar jobs, you are no longer guessing what people want. You know, with certainty, because they handed you money for it. The product you should build is sitting inside that pile of validated work, and your only job is to recognize it and package it.

> **KEY IDEA** Do not invent a product. Extract one. The thing you have delivered over and over as a service is a product the market has already validated and priced for you. Inventing is a bet. Extracting is collecting on a sure thing.

This is the entire reason the ladder is built in this order. The passive-first crowd has to guess what to build, and most guess wrong and quit. You get to skip the guessing, because Book Two was a paid research project into exactly this question, and the answers are in your Library.

What "productizing" actually means

> **PLAIN ENGLISH** To productize is to take the repeatable value you deliver as a service and package it so it can be sold many times without you doing the work each time. The service trades your hours for money. The product breaks that trade. You build it once and it sells again and again.

That broken trade is leverage, the term from Chapter 3, and it is the whole point of this rung. A service has a ceiling made of your hours. A product does not. The same skill, the same lane, the same validated work, repackaged so that selling the hundredth copy costs you nothing.

How to spot the product inside your service

Four signals point straight at the product hiding in your work. Look for them in your System Library and your client history.

Repetition. What do you deliver again and again, in roughly the same shape, for different clients? The thing you are tired of rebuilding from scratch is your strongest product candidate, because repetition is proof of demand.

The reusable core. Inside any delivery, some of it is custom to the client and some of it is the same every time, your framework, your structure, your process, your starting templates. That same-every-time core is the productizable asset. You have already built it. It lives in your Library.

The transferable knowledge. What do clients keep asking you to explain? What do they wish they could do themselves? Recurring questions are a course or a guide asking to be written, because they reveal a thing many people want to learn and will pay to be taught.

The tedious but valuable. What part of your work is genuinely valuable but a grind to do? That is a candidate for a tool or template that lets others skip the grind, the same grind you would happily have paid to skip when you started.

Run those four filters over your work and you will rarely find nothing. More often you will find several products, and the problem becomes choosing, which is a far better problem than inventing from a blank page.

The same work, packaged for more or less leverage

Once you have spotted the validated thing, you have a choice about how to package it, and the choice is a tradeoff between price and scale.

From Hours to Leverage

The same validated work, packaged at different points on the leverage curve.

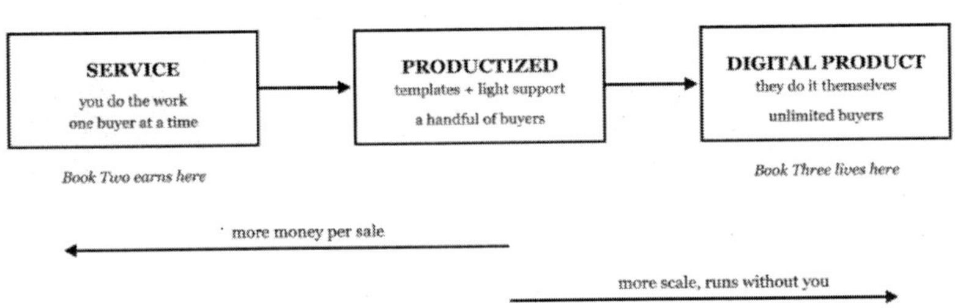

You are not inventing a product. You are repackaging work the market already validated.

The same validated work can be sold at different points on a leverage curve. On the left sits the pure service you already run: highest price per sale, but zero leverage, because it costs you your hours and serves one buyer at a time. On the right sits the pure digital product, a template, a course, a tool: a low price per sale, but unlimited leverage, because the buyer does the work themselves and you can sell to everyone at once while you sleep. In the middle sits the productized service, templates plus a little support, which splits the difference.

There is no single correct spot. More "done for you" means more money per sale and less scale. More "do it yourself" means less per sale and far more scale. Most operators end up offering more than one point on this curve, a premium done-for-you tier and a cheaper do-it-yourself product, capturing buyers at different budgets from the same body of work. The point of the diagram is simply this: you are not choosing a different business, you are repackaging the one you have, and you get to decide how far toward leverage you want to push.

Here is how that extraction looks across a few common lanes.

The service you deliver	The repeatable core	The product you extract
Writing email welcome sequences	Your proven sequence structure and templates	A template pack buyers fill in themselves
Running content audits	Your audit checklist and scoring method	A self-audit toolkit, or a short course teaching it
Setting up systems for clients	Your standard setup and configuration	A downloadable kit with step-by-step setup
Explaining the same skill repeatedly	The knowledge clients keep asking for	A focused course or guide

Notice that in every row, the product is not a new idea. It is the same-every-time core of work you are already paid to do, lifted out and packaged.

Extract beats invent, and it is not close

REALITY CHECK "I'll build a product around whatever's trending, that's where the money is." That is the bet that empties bank accounts and fills the internet with unsold courses. A trend tells you what is loud, not what your specific buyers will pay you for. Your validated service tells you exactly what a real audience already values, because they already bought it from you. Build your first product from your own service work, not from a trend you read about. The trend is a stranger's guess. Your service history is your own proof.

This is the single biggest advantage you carry onto this rung, and it is worth pausing to feel it. The hardest part of building a product, knowing whether anyone wants it, is already solved for you. You are not launching into silence and hoping. You are packaging something a paying audience has already told you they want.

Start with the smallest sellable version

One discipline before we leave this chapter, because it saves the conscientious from the most expensive product mistake.

Do not disappear for six months to build the perfect, enormous course before you sell a thing. That is the passive-first valley sneaking back in through the side door. Instead, build the smallest version of your validated product that someone could actually buy, a single template pack, a short guide, one focused tool. Get it in front of buyers, confirm it sells, and only then expand it. You validated your lane cheaply in Chapter 4 and you will validate your product the same way. Small, real, and selling beats big, perfect, and untested every time.

And keep your service running while you build. Remember from Chapter 3 that you climb the rungs, you do not abandon them. Your services pay the bills during the build, and they keep feeding you fresh product ideas, because every new client is more market research you are getting paid to conduct.

What's next

You now know that your first product is hiding in your service work, how to spot it, and how to decide where on the leverage curve to package it. The next question is the specific form: of all the products you could extract, which one should you build first, and what does each form actually cost you to make versus what it can return. Chapter 10 is the honest menu, matching product types to your skills with the effort and reward laid out plainly, so you build the right thing first instead of the most exciting thing.

> **TRY THIS** Open your System Library and your list of completed client work. Run the four signals over it: which deliverable have you repeated most, what is its reusable core, what do clients keep asking you to explain, and what valuable task do you dread repeating. Pick the single strongest product candidate. Write one sentence describing the smallest sellable version of it, and mark where on the leverage curve you would package it first. That sentence is your Book Three starting point, and it is built from work the market already paid you to validate.

Chapter 10
What to Build
(Matching Products to Your Skills)

You know what you are going to sell, because you extracted it from validated work in the last chapter. What you have not decided is what form it takes. The same validated value can become a template, a tool, a course, and more, and those forms are not interchangeable. Each one costs a different amount to build and pays back differently, and choosing the wrong form is how people either bury months in something too big or settle for something that earns too little.

This chapter is the honest menu. I will lay out the real options, what each costs you to build, what each returns, and which one you should almost certainly build first.

The menu

There are five product forms a one-person, AI-leveraged operator can realistically build. Here is each one, plainly.

Templates and kits. Packaged versions of your reusable core, the frameworks, swipe files, checklists, and starting documents you already use to deliver. The buyer fills them in or follows them. These are the fastest to build, because you are mostly cleaning up and packaging what already exists in your System Library. Lower price per sale, but excellent margin and almost no build time. For most people, this is the right first product.

The productized service. The middle of the leverage curve from Chapter 9: a fixed-scope package, often templates plus a bit of your support or customization. Easy to start because it is close to the service you already run, and it sells at a healthy price. Less scalable, because it still involves some of your time, but a natural and low-risk first step out of pure services.

Courses and guides. The transferable knowledge clients keep asking you for, packaged as something they can learn from. Scalable and potentially high return, but it costs real effort to build well, and it demands a specific skill: you have to be able to teach, not just do. If explaining things clearly is a strength, this is powerful. If it is not, a course will expose that fast.

Tools and apps. Something that does the work for the buyer: a calculator, a custom assistant, a working mini-application. These can command higher prices and feel stickier, because they deliver ongoing utility. They also cost the most to build and maintain, and the bar rises sharply if real technical work is involved. AI lowers that bar somewhat, but a tool is still the heaviest lift on this list.

Memberships and subscriptions. Recurring access to content, tools, or community. The highest long-term leverage, because the income repeats, but the hardest thing to start cold, because it demands an ongoing flow of value and usually an existing audience to fill it. This is almost never a first product. It is where you go later, once you have an audience and proven products to build it around.

PLAIN ENGLISH Recurring revenue is income that repeats on its own, like a monthly subscription, instead of being earned one sale at a time. It is the most powerful kind of income and the hardest to start, which is exactly why it belongs later on the climb, not at the beginning.

Effort against return, and where to start

Lay those five forms on two axes, what they cost you to build against what they can return, and the right first move becomes obvious.

What to Build First

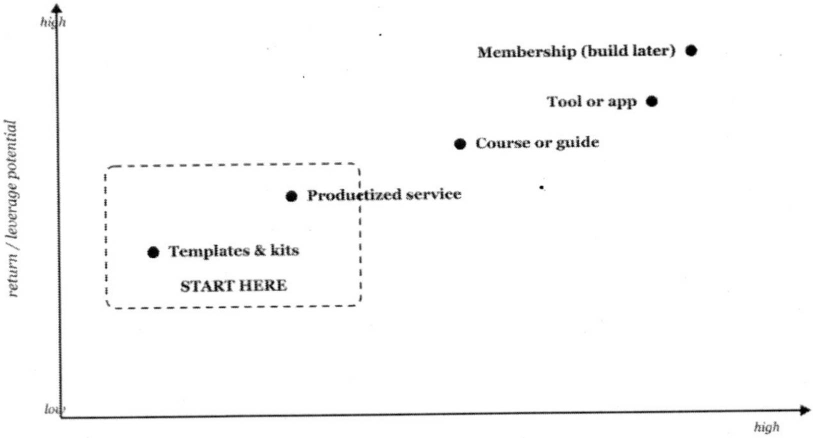

Start low-effort for a fast win and proof. Climb to higher-effort, higher-return once you have both.

The instinct is to chase the top of the return axis, the course, the tool, the membership. Resist it as a first move. Your first product is not about maximizing theoretical return. It is about getting a real product built, listed, and selling fast, so you get the same thing services gave you: an early win, proof the format works, and cash to fund the next build. That argues for the low-effort end of the chart, the start-here zone, where templates and productized services live. They are quick to build, quick to test, and they return well for the effort.

Then you climb, exactly as you climbed onto this rung in the first place. Once a low-effort product proves it sells and funds your time, you build up and to the right: the guide, the course, the tool, eventually the membership. Each higher-effort product is a safer bet by then, because the earlier ones proved your audience buys and taught you what they want more of.

> **KEY IDEA** Your first product should be the lowest-effort packaging of your validated core that still delivers real value. Build it fast, prove it sells, bank the win, and use it to fund the higher-effort, higher-return products. Do not open with your magnum opus.

Match the form to you, not just to the return

The chart shows return potential, but potential is not the same as your result. The right first product sits where three things meet, and you will recognize this logic from how you chose your lane in Chapter 4.

It has to be a form you can actually execute well. A course is worthless if you cannot teach, no matter how high its return potential. A tool stalls if it is beyond what you can build and maintain. Templates and kits, by contrast, fit almost anyone, because if you can deliver the service, you can package its core.

It has to be a form whose effort you can afford right now. The best product you never finish earns nothing. Pick something you can complete and ship while your services keep the lights on, not something that requires you to disappear for a season.

And it has to carry the validated value from Chapter 9. The form changes how the value is delivered. It does not get to change what the value is. Whatever you build, it must still be the thing your buyers already proved they want.

Where those three meet is your first product. For most readers, most of the time, that intersection is a template, a kit, or a productized service. That is not settling. That is starting smart.

The honest comparison

Here is the menu with the tradeoffs side by side, so you can choose with your eyes open.

Product form	What it is	Build effort	Return and scale	Good first product?
Templates & kits	Your reusable core, packaged	Low	Modest price, high margin, scales fully	Yes, for almost anyone
Productized service	Fixed package, templates plus light support	Low to medium	Healthy price, limited scale	Yes, a natural first step

Course or guide	Your knowledge, taught	Medium to high	High, if you can teach and have reach	Later, unless teaching is your strength
Tool or app	Something that does the work	High	High, sticky, higher price	Later
Membership	Recurring access or community	High, ongoing	Highest long-term, recurring	Much later, needs an audience

Read the right column as one instruction: start at the top of the table, climb toward the bottom over time.

REALITY CHECK "I'm going to build the complete, definitive course as my first product." This is the most common and most expensive product mistake there is. You pour months into a large, polished thing before you have any proof the format sells or any cash coming in, which is the passive-first valley wearing a new costume. Build the small thing first. A template pack that sells this month teaches you more, and funds you better, than a magnum opus that launches to silence next year. You can always build the big course later, on a foundation of proof, with money in the bank and an audience that has already bought from you.

What's next

You have chosen your product and its form, matched to your skills and to an effort you can afford, carrying value the market already validated. Now you build it, and you build it the way an operator does: fast, using AI, without producing the kind of slop that gets refunded and one-starred. Creating quickly without creating junk is its own discipline, and Chapter 11 is how you hold both at once.

TRY THIS Take the product candidate and the smallest-sellable-version sentence you wrote at the end of Chapter 9. Now choose its form using this chapter's menu, and run it through the three-way match: is this a form I can execute well, can I afford the effort to finish it soon, and does it still deliver the validated value. If your first instinct was a big course or a complex tool, deliberately ask whether a template, kit, or productized service could deliver the same value far faster. Write down the final form and the smallest complete version of it you could ship within a few weeks. That is what you will build in the next chapter.

Chapter 11
Creating It Fast Without Creating Slop

You have a product to build and the smallest complete version of it in mind. Now you make it, and this is where the stakes quietly rise.

A service goes to one client. A product is built once and sold to everyone, which means its quality compounds across every buyer you will ever have. Get it right and every sale earns another good review and another referral. Get it wrong and you have built a slop machine that generates refunds and one-star reviews at scale, automatically, for as long as it is listed. AI makes building fast. It also makes building slop fast. This chapter is about holding both ropes, speed and substance, with the exact prompts to do it.

The disease of this entire category

Walk through any marketplace of AI-related products and you will see the sickness everywhere: thin, padded, generic products generated in an afternoon and dressed up to look like more. The hundred-page guide that should have been ten pages. The thousand-prompt pack where most are filler. Buyers have grown allergic to it, and their allergy is your opening, because a product with real substance now stands out violently. Being the substantial one is not just the ethical choice. It is the commercially smart one, because it earns the reviews and word of mouth the slop never will.

The two ways a product goes wrong

The first and most common is thin and padded: you let AI generate volume and ship something that looks substantial and is mostly air. AI makes this the path of least resistance, which is why you must consciously refuse it. The second is over-building: adding length and modules nobody asked for, polishing forever, never shipping. The operator builds neither. You build the smallest complete thing that fully delivers the validated result, substantial in value, lean in size. Small is not the enemy. Empty is.

Depth, not length

Same topic, two products. Which one earns the five-star review?

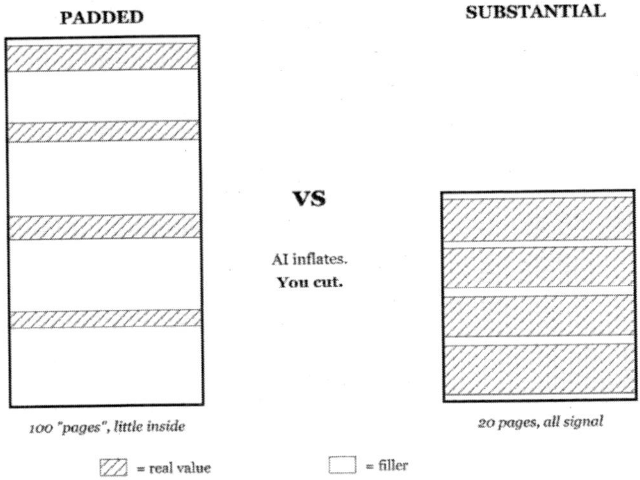

The buyer paid for the result, not the word count. Cut everything that does not serve it.

A product is judged by the result it delivers, not its size. Two products can cover the same topic, the padded one five times longer, while the lean one is the one that actually gets the buyer the outcome. AI's natural tendency is to inflate, because filling space is effortless for it. Your job is the opposite.

KEY IDEA Judge your product by the result it delivers, never by its length. AI inflates; you cut. A lean product that gets the buyer the outcome beats a padded one that buries it, every time. Depth is the differentiator. Length is the trap.

Where the substance comes from

The secret to building fast and substantial at once is where you get the substance, and the answer is: not from AI. Your product's substance is your validated method, the thing your service clients already paid you for, sitting in your System Library. AI is the production engine that turns that method into a finished product fast. The thinking is yours. The typing is shared.

A thin product	A substantial product
Substance comes from AI's general knowledge	Substance comes from your validated method
Padded to look big	Lean and dense with value

Generic, could be anyone's	Carries your specific experience and examples
Gets the buyer no real result	Actually delivers the outcome
Earns refunds and one-star reviews	Earns referrals and repeat buyers

REALITY CHECK "I'll just have AI write the whole product." Then you have built slop. AI's "substance" is an average of what already exists, the same generic material every other AI-generated product is made of. The more of the thinking you hand to the machine, the thinner and more generic your product becomes, because you removed the one thing that made it worth buying: you. Use AI to produce your method faster. Never use it to replace your method.

The build, step by step

Outline from your own method first, before you touch AI. This skeleton is the substance, and building it yourself guarantees the product is yours. Use this structure.

TEMPLATE — The method-first product skeleton THE RESULT THE BUYER REACHES: [the outcome] WHO IT IS FOR, AND THEIR STARTING POINT: [buyer] THE STEPS, in order, from your own validated method: Step 1: [what they do] / my real example: [***] / the common mistake here:*** [] Step 2: [what they do] / my real example: [***] / the common mistake here:*** [] Step 3: [...] WHAT THEY HAVE AT THE END: [the finished result] Write this from your own work on a blank page. Do not open ChatGPT until it is done.

Then fill it with AI for speed. Hand it the skeleton and let it draft each part, but hold it to your structure.

PROMPT — Expand your own outline "I am building a [product type] for [buyer]. Here is my outline, which is my own validated method: [paste your skeleton]. For each point, draft the content at the level of detail a buyer needs to actually do it. Keep my structure and my method exactly. Do NOT add new sections or topics, and do NOT pad. Where a step needs an example, leave [MY EXAMPLE HERE] so I can drop in my own. Plain and direct, no filler, no hype."

The bans are doing the work: no new topics, no padding, leave space for my examples. That keeps AI in the production seat and you in the substance seat.

Build in your real examples where you left the markers. Your specific cases and before-and-afters are your fingerprint and the thing AI cannot fake.

Then make the substance cut, because the draft will be longer than it should be.

PROMPT — The substance cut "Here is a section of my product: [paste]. Act as a ruthless editor whose only goal is signal-to-noise. Quote every sentence or paragraph that does not directly help the buyer reach the result, the filler, the throat-clearing, the generic advice they already know, the repetition, the hedging, and for each say why it should go. Do not rewrite anything longer, and do not praise it. Just show me what to cut."

Then check it stands alone.

> **PLAIN ENGLISH** Self-contained means the buyer can reach the full result using only the product, without needing you to explain or fill gaps. A product is sold without you in the room, so anything it leaves unsaid is a hole the buyer falls into, and then reviews.

PROMPT — Find the gaps "Here is my full product draft: [paste or summarize]. A buyer will use this with no access to me. Point out every place where a beginner in [buyer]'s position would get stuck, hit an unexplained assumption, or need information I did not give. List the gaps, do not fill them."

Finally, verify and test. Run the accuracy check from Chapter 8 over any factual claims, because a product repeats its errors to every buyer who opens it. Then give it to one real person in your audience and watch whether they reach the result, the same cheap validation you used for your lane and offer.

A worked example: padding cut to signal

Here is what the expand prompt might produce for a section on subject lines in our welcome-email product, before you cut it:

"Subject lines are one of the most important parts of any email, and it is really crucial to get them right because they are the first thing your subscriber sees. In today's fast-paced digital world, people receive countless emails every single day, so standing out in a crowded inbox has never been more important. A great subject line can make all the difference between an email that gets opened and one that gets ignored. There are many different strategies you can use to write compelling subject lines that grab attention..."

Run the substance-cut prompt on it and the verdict is that nearly all of it is air: "one of the most important parts," "in today's fast-paced world," "countless emails every single day," all of it throat-clearing the buyer already knows and skips. Here is the operator's version after the cut:

"Your subject line has one job: earn the open. For a welcome email, lead with the reward they signed up for, not your brand. 'Your 10% code is inside' beats 'Welcome to Maple & Stone,' because it leads with what they want, not who you are."

Forty-some words replace eighty, and the short version is the one that actually teaches a buyer to write a better subject line in the next minute. That is depth beating length, and it is the difference between a five-star product and a refund.

The honesty of an AI-built product

A product that is genuinely your validated method, written up with AI's help, is your work, and you can sell it with a clear conscience. A product where AI supplied the thinking and you supplied a cover is the slop this chapter exists to prevent, and no disclosure label fixes that. The line is not whether AI helped. It is whether the substance is yours. Keep the substance yours and the question answers itself.

What's next

You have built a lean, substantial product carrying your validated method, gap-checked and tested on a real person. Now comes the part the title promised and the part most misunderstood: selling it on autopilot, and the honest truth about what "passive" actually means once the product is live. Chapter 12 closes Book Three by separating the real mechanics of selling without your hours from the fantasy that products sell themselves.

> **TRY THIS** Before you open ChatGPT, fill in the method-first skeleton from your own validated work, on a blank page. That is your substance and it must come from you. Then run the expand prompt to draft it fast, and drop your real examples into the markers. Run the substance-cut prompt section by section and actually make the cuts, even the ones AI wanted to keep. Run the gap prompt and close the holes. Verify any claims, then hand it to one real person and watch them use it. What remains, lean and dense and unmistakably yours, is the smallest complete version of your product. Save every prompt and the skeleton to your System Library, because your next product will start from them.

Chapter 12
Selling on Autopilot
(The Honest Truth About "Passive")

You have a product. Lean, substantial, tested, carrying your validated method. Now you sell it without trading your hours for each sale, which is the promise on the cover and the reason you climbed this far. But before the mechanics, I owe you the most honest paragraph in the book, because this is the exact spot where the fantasy version of passive income has wrecked more people than any other.

A product does not sell itself. "Set it and forget it" is a lie. What is true, and better, is "set it up, then tend it." The income becomes passive. The selling never becomes magic. Understand that difference and you will build something real. Believe the fantasy and you will list a product, hear crickets, and conclude the whole thing was a scam, when the only thing that failed was an expectation nobody should have sold you.

What "passive" actually means

Here is the honest accounting, and it is the heart of this chapter.

> **KEY IDEA** "Passive" describes the income, not the business. The sale itself can run on its own, around the clock, while you sleep. Getting buyers to that sale cannot. The work does not disappear when you reach this rung. It changes shape, from doing the work per client to building and tending the system that sells. Less work over time, never zero work. That is the real, earned version, and it is the one that lasts.

This is not a downgrade of the dream. It is the dream made survivable. A business that needs zero attention does not exist, and chasing one is how people quit. A business whose income increasingly outruns the effort that feeds it absolutely exists, and that is what you are building.

Selling needs two things, and beginners forget one

To sell a product you need two things: a place where the sale happens, and a way for buyers to find it. The product existing is necessary and nowhere near sufficient. Beginners obsess over the first and ignore the second, and the second is where almost all the failure lives.

REALITY CHECK "If I build a great product, people will come." They will not. "Build it and they will come" is the single most expensive belief in this entire field. The internet is not a small town where a good shop gets noticed. It is an infinite shelf, and a product nobody is driving traffic to is invisible, no matter how good it is. Most products do not fail because they are bad. They fail because nobody ever sees them. Plan for traffic before you fall in love with the product.

The storefront: keep it boring

You need somewhere the transaction happens: a simple sales page, a listing on a marketplace, a basic platform that takes payment and delivers the file. That is it. Do not spend three weeks building an elaborate website before you have sold a single copy. The simplest thing that can take money and hand over the product is the right thing to start with, because the storefront is not your constraint. Traffic is. Specific platforms change and the companion resource keeps current options, but the principle does not: pick the boring, fast option and move on to the part that matters.

When you do write the sales page, AI gets you a strong first draft fast.

PROMPT — Draft your sales page "Help me write a simple sales page for a digital product. The product: [paste its result, who it is for, and what the buyer gets]. My one-sentence offer: [paste]. Write a short page with: a headline naming the result, two or three lines on the problem it solves, a clear list of what is inside, who it is for, and one clear call to action. Lead with the buyer's outcome, be specific, and use no hype words and no fake urgency. Mark [PROOF HERE] where I should add a testimonial or sample."

Then you do the operator's pass: make it specific, true, and yours, and drop real proof into the marker.

Traffic: the part that is actually work

"Passive" describes the sale, not getting them to it.

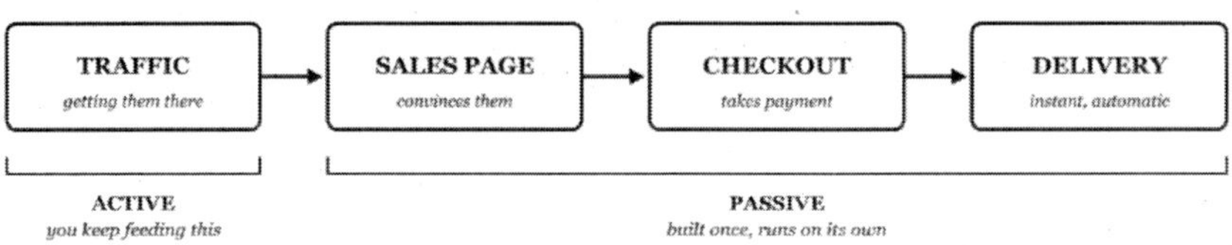

Most products don't fail because they're bad. They fail because nobody sees them.

Look at the diagram, because it is the whole truth of this rung on one line. The sale, the page, the checkout, the delivery: all of that is passive once built. It runs on its own. The one part that is not passive is the front, getting people to the page, and that is where your ongoing effort goes from here. The good news is that the effort is leveraged: drive one visitor or a thousand to the same page, and the page does identical work for free. Your job is the traffic. The machine does the selling.

Here is where your first traffic comes from, in order of how easy it is.

Start with the people who already trust you. Your past and current service clients are your warmest possible buyers, and they are the first the flywheel from Chapter 8 hands you. Tell them you built a product.

TEMPLATE — Launch to people who already know you Hi [name], a while back I [worked with you on / helped you with] [the service]. I have just put together a [product] that [delivers the result], so people can get [the value] without [the cost or wait of the full service]. Thought of you, and of anyone you know who is dealing with [the problem]. Here it is, no pressure: [link]. Glad to answer any questions.

Next, the channels you have already been building, the communities you are useful in and any audience you are growing. Then content that compounds, which is the closest thing to genuinely semi-passive traffic that exists: useful pieces that attract your buyers over time and keep working long after you publish them. It takes real effort up front and pays back slowly, which is exactly why most people skip it and why it works for those who do not.

PROMPT — Content that attracts buyers "I sell [product] to [buyer]. Suggest five pieces of genuinely useful content that would attract [buyer] by helping them with [the problem], where each piece stands on its own as real help AND naturally leads to my product. For each, give the topic and the single real takeaway it must deliver. No clickbait, and nothing that is just a thinly veiled ad."

A warning attached to that prompt, because it is the spam trap from Chapter 7 in a new outfit: content that is a thin ad wearing a hat fools no one and attracts no one. The content has to genuinely help, or it does not compound. Substance again, the same rule as the product itself.

Paid traffic, ads, can work and is fast, but it costs money and skill, and it punishes a page that does not yet convert. Treat it as a later lever you pull once the page sells reliably to free traffic, not as a way to rescue a product that is not selling.

What is passive and what is not

Keep this honest split in front of you, because confusing the two columns is how people both overpromise to themselves and underbuild the part that matters.

Runs on its own (passive)	Needs you (active)
The sales page, once written	Driving traffic to it
The checkout and payment	Keeping the product current

Instant delivery of the file	Answering buyer questions
The product itself	Marketing and content

You can shrink the right column over time, and you should. AI can draft your buyer-question responses into a reusable FAQ. Content you wrote keeps pulling traffic. Past buyers refer new ones. The active work never hits zero, but it does steadily fall as a share of the income, and that downward slope is what "passive" honestly means.

The earned version is the better version

Here is why none of this should disappoint you. The fantasy version of passive income, money for nothing, forever, does not exist and never did. What you are building is sturdier than the fantasy: a selling system that runs while you sleep, fed by traffic that increasingly compounds on work you already did, around a product the market already validated. Over time it asks less of you and pays more reliably, and because it is built on real value and real demand, it does not collapse the way the get-rich-quick version always does. You traded a lie that pays nothing for a truth that pays for years.

The end of Book Three

You now have the leverage rung. A product that sells without your hours, through a storefront you keep simple and a traffic engine you feed and steadily automate. Combined with the service business beneath it, you have two of the three rungs running: cash and market intelligence from services, leverage and increasingly passive income from products.

What remains is to make the whole machine run without you standing in the middle of every step, and to stack these pieces so they reinforce each other into something that genuinely changes your life. That is automation, the top rung, and it is Book Four. Chapter 13 starts where every honest automation effort must: with what to automate, and just as importantly, what to never touch.

TRY THIS Do the smallest complete version of selling. Set up the boring storefront, the simplest thing that takes payment and delivers your product. Write the sales page with the prompt, then make it specific and true and add your real proof. Then pick exactly one traffic source to start, and make it the warmest one: send the launch message to your past and current clients today. Do not build five traffic channels at once, and do not touch paid ads yet. One storefront, one page, one warm traffic source, one real send. Save the prompts and your sales page to your System Library, because your next product will reuse all of it.

Chapter 13
Automating the Boring 80%

You have two rungs running, and you are standing in the middle of every step of both. Every service delivered, every product sold, every question answered, you are there. That is the ceiling this rung exists to break. Automation is how the machine starts running without you in the center of it, which is what turns a business that owns you into one you own.

But automation is the rung that punishes impatience and carelessness hardest, so Book Four opens with the two rules that keep it from blowing up in your face: what to automate, and what to never touch. Get those right and automation sets you free. Get them wrong and you build a fast, tireless machine for producing mistakes.

First, the prerequisite

One sentence, because Chapter 3 already made the case: you automate a business that works, not a wish. Automation scales whatever you point it at. Point it at a proven service and a selling product and it multiplies them. Point it at something that does not work yet and you have automated chaos. You earned this rung the right way, with two working rungs beneath it, so you have something real to automate. Good. Proceed.

The principle
automate the boring 80%, protect the 20%

Most of your working time goes to a large pile of repetitive, low-judgment tasks: scheduling, formatting, reminders, answering the same questions, moving files around, basic admin. That is the boring 80%, and it is where automation belongs. A much smaller share of your time goes to the work that actually creates value and only you can do: the final judgment on quality, the client relationships, the pricing calls, the taste. That is your 20%, and it is precisely what you must protect from automation, because it is your entire edge.

> **KEY IDEA** Automate the boring 80%, the repetitive low-judgment work that drains your time. Protect the 20% that needs your judgment, taste, trust, and accountability, because that is the part with the value and the part AI cannot do. Automation should free you to spend more time on your 20%, never replace it.

Match the automation to the judgment

Automation is not all-or-nothing. It has levels, and the right level for any task depends on one thing: how much judgment the task requires.

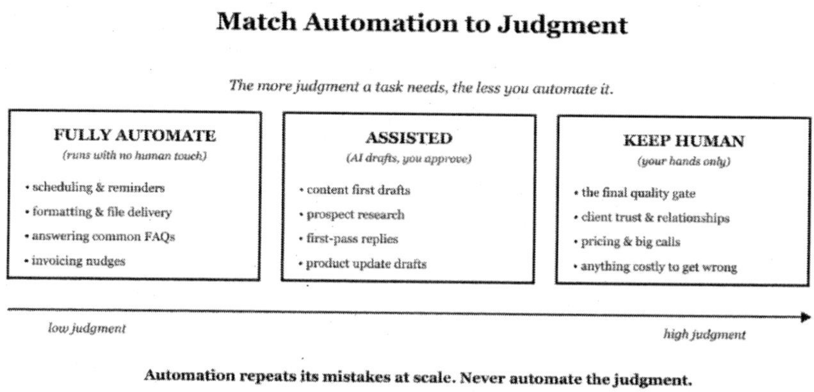

At the low-judgment end sit rules-based, repetitive, safe tasks: scheduling, formatting, reminders, common FAQs. These you can fully automate, hands-off, because there is little judgment to lose and little harm if they run on their own. In the middle sit tasks AI can do most of but that need your eyes before they go out: content drafts, prospect research, first-pass replies. These you make assisted, not autonomous. At the high-judgment end sit the things that are your actual job: the final quality gate, client trust, pricing, anything costly to get wrong. These you keep fully human.

PLAIN ENGLISH Human in the loop means the automation does the work but a person approves it before it takes effect. It is the safe middle setting: you get most of the speed of automation while keeping the judgment that catches mistakes. For anything that could reach a client or buyer, this is your default, not full automation.

Why the judgment line is not negotiable

Here is the danger that makes the diagram's rule absolute.

REALITY CHECK "If automating saves time, I should automate as much as possible." No. Automation runs without you, which means a bad automated step repeats its mistake on every client and buyer it touches, silently, until you notice. A human doing the wrong thing makes one mistake. An automation doing the wrong thing makes a thousand, while you sleep. The more judgment a task needs, the more a mistake costs, and the less you should automate it. Over-automation does not scale your business. It scales your errors and quietly automates away the human edge people were paying you for.

This is the same compounding logic from the product chapter, now applied to your whole operation. Leverage cuts both ways. The thing that multiplies your output multiplies your mistakes just as efficiently, so you only fully hand over the tasks where a mistake is cheap and rare.

Find your boring 80%

You cannot automate what you have not named. Start by getting your recurring work out of your head and onto a list, then sort it. ChatGPT is a fast, dispassionate sorter.

PROMPT — Audit and classify your tasks "Here is how I spend my working time across my service and product business: [list your recurring tasks]. Sort each into one of three buckets: FULLY AUTOMATE (rules-based, repetitive, low judgment, safe if it runs without me), ASSISTED (AI can draft it but I must approve before it goes out), or KEEP HUMAN (needs my judgment, taste, trust, or carries real risk if it is wrong). For anything you put in FULLY AUTOMATE, name the one risk to watch. Be conservative: if a mistake would reach a client or buyer, it is not fully-automate."

The conservative instruction is deliberate. AI, asked to find efficiencies, will happily over-automate, so you bias it the other way and make it justify every hands-off call. Use it to draft the sort, then apply your own judgment, because where the line falls is itself a judgment call, and that one is yours.

TEMPLATE — Your task audit Task: [name it] How often: [daily / weekly / per client / per sale] Judgment it needs: [low / medium / high] Bucket: [fully automate / assisted / keep human] If automated, the risk to watch: [what a silent mistake here would cost]

Work down your list, and your automation plan writes itself: the fully-automate rows first, the assisted rows next, the keep-human rows left alone on purpose.

Build the automation, assisted by default

For most tasks, building the automation means creating a reusable asset that does most of the work and leaves you the approval. Take the repetitive thing and turn it into something that runs.

PROMPT — Turn a repetitive task into a reusable asset "I keep doing the same task over and over: [describe it, and paste examples of how I currently do it, such as the buyer questions I keep answering and my answers]. Draft a reusable asset that lets me handle this near-instantly in my own voice, for example a set of canned responses, a checklist, or a fill-in template. Flag any case inside this task that actually needs a human judgment call rather than a canned approach, so I keep those manual."

Notice the last instruction: even inside a task you are automating, it pulls out the parts that still need you. That is the whole discipline in miniature. Automate the rule-following core, keep the judgment calls.

The two things people automate that they should not

Beyond the judgment line, two specific over-automations kill businesses, and both are worth naming so you avoid them.

The over-automation	What goes wrong	The fix
Automating the final quality gate	Mistakes ship to every buyer at once	Keep the gate human, always
Automating the client relationship	People feel they are talking to a bot, trust dies	Automate the admin around the relationship, never the relationship
Setting it up and never checking it	It breaks or drifts silently and you find out from a complaint	Schedule a regular review of every automation
Automating before the business works	You scale chaos efficiently	Fix the process by hand first, then automate it

The relationship one deserves emphasis. The trust and human connection with your clients and buyers is not overhead to be optimized away. It is a chunk of what they are paying for, especially at the service rung. Automate the reminders, the scheduling, the formatting that surrounds the relationship. Never automate the relationship itself, or you will have efficiently removed the reason people chose you over a faceless competitor.

Check what you automate

One last discipline. An automation is not "set and forget," it is "set and review." Things break. Inputs change. A response that was fine six months ago reads wrong today. Put a recurring check on your calendar to look at every automation and confirm it is still doing what you think. The silent failure, the automation that quietly stopped working or started doing the wrong thing while you assumed it was fine, is the most common way automated systems hurt you.

A quick worked example

Say the same five questions arrive from buyers of your welcome-email product, over and over: how to install the emails, whether they work on a given platform, how to customize them, your refund terms, and whether you offer the done-for-you service too. You run the audit prompt and four of those land in FULLY AUTOMATE: they are factual, rules-based, and safe as canned answers, so they become an instant auto-response or FAQ. But the fifth, the one asking about your done-for-you service, you deliberately keep human, because it is a sales conversation with a warm buyer, exactly the high-value relationship moment you never hand to a bot. You automated the boring four and protected the one that could turn into a service sale. That is the boring 80% and the precious 20%, sorted correctly.

What's next

You know what to automate, what to keep, and how to match the level to the judgment. The next question is how to actually run all the functions a whole team would normally handle, marketing, operations, content, admin, as one person with AI doing the heavy lifting. That is your one-person back office, and Chapter 14 builds it.

> **TRY THIS** List your recurring tasks and run the audit prompt to sort them into the three buckets, then fill in the task-audit template for your top five time-drains. Pick exactly one low-judgment task to fully automate and one medium task to make assisted, and build the first one this week using the reusable-asset prompt. For the assisted one, set the rule now: AI drafts, you approve, every time. And put one recurring date on your calendar to review whatever you automate. Save the prompts and your task audit to your System Library. You have started turning a business you run into a business that runs.

Chapter 14
Your One-Person AI Back Office

A real business is not just the work it sells. Behind the product or service sits a whole machine: marketing to attract people, sales to convert them, operations to deliver, support to answer questions, and admin to keep the money and the calendar straight. In a normal company, each of those is a person or a department. You are going to run all of them, alone, with AI doing the heavy lifting in each.

This is the chapter where you stop thinking of yourself as a freelancer with tasks and start running like a small company with one employee who happens to be everywhere at once. That shift is what makes the top rung possible.

You are the operator, not the staff

PLAIN ENGLISH Your back office is all the supporting functions that keep the business running: marketing, sales, support, admin, the operations around the work. It is everything except the core value you personally deliver. Running a back office does not mean doing all of it by hand. It means making sure all of it happens.

The mental move is to stop seeing a to-do list and start seeing functions. Each function is a role a team would normally fill, and AI lets you fill it. You are not the marketing person, the support person, and the bookkeeper, drowning in three jobs. You are the operator who directs all three, with AI doing the labor inside each, at the automation level Chapter 13 taught you to choose.

Notice the shape. You sit at the center, holding the one thing that cannot be delegated or automated: judgment and accountability. Around you are the functions, each run with AI assistance at a different level. Support is mostly automated. Admin is automated. Marketing is assisted. Sales is assisted but you make the close. Delivery stays your human-kept core. One person, at the center, running what used to take a team.

> **KEY IDEA** Run your business like a company where AI fills the roles. Your job is to orchestrate the functions, not to labor inside every one. The day you are doing all the work in every function by hand is the day you have built a job, not a business. The operator directs. The back office runs.

What stays yours in each function

Automation level is not the same as abdication. Even in a heavily automated function, something stays human, and knowing what keeps you from automating away your edge.

Function	What AI handles	What you keep
Marketing & content	Drafting, repurposing, scheduling posts	The strategy and the substance, what to say and why
Sales	Research, drafting outreach and proposals	The relationship and the close
Delivery / ops	Producing first drafts of the work	The quality gate and final judgment
Support	Answering common, factual questions	The judgment calls and the sales conversations
Admin & finance	Tracking, reminders, scheduling	The decisions about money and priorities

Read the right column and you will see it is the same thing every time: judgment, relationships, and accountability. That is your job now. Everything else, you staff with AI.

Running the functions: the content engine

You already have the tools for several functions. Sales runs on the offer and outreach prompts from Chapters 6 and 7. Delivery runs through the quality gate from Chapter 8. Support runs on the reusable FAQ from Chapter 13. The two functions that need new tooling here are marketing and admin, because they are what most one-person operators neglect until the business stalls.

Marketing, for you, means a content engine: a way to produce a steady stream of genuinely useful content without it eating your life. The trick is to get many pieces from one idea.

PROMPT — The content engine "I run a [business] for [buyer] and want a steady stream of content that attracts them. Take this one core idea or lesson from my actual work: [paste the idea]. Turn it into a week of content: [number] short posts and one longer piece, each delivering a real, usable takeaway on its own, and each pointing naturally toward [my offer or product]. Be specific and genuinely useful. No clickbait, no thin ads dressed up as content. Give me the angle and the single key point for each piece."

The substance rule from Chapters 11 and 12 applies here too: the content has to genuinely help, or it does not attract anyone. AI multiplies one real idea into a week of pieces. It cannot supply the idea. The core lesson comes from your work, the same way your product's substance did.

Running the functions: the admin layer

Admin is the function people most love to ignore and most regret ignoring, because it is where money slips through cracks and clients fall through gaps. The fix is not a complicated system. It is one simple, minimal place to see the state of your business.

PROMPT — Set up a minimal tracking system "Help me set up a simple tracking system for my one-person business. I need to stay on top of: prospects I have contacted, active client work and its status, product sales, invoices owed to me, and content I have scheduled. Design a minimal structure, the fields or columns I need, that I can keep in one place. Then tell me the few things I should check once a week so nothing falls through the cracks. Keep it lean. I am one person, not a corporation."

Resist the urge to build an elaborate system. A one-person business needs a one-person system: minimal, glanceable, enough to catch what matters and nothing more.

The operating rhythm that holds it together

A back office full of functions does not run on heroics. It runs on rhythm. The operators who do not burn out are the ones who batch their work and run on a repeating weekly cadence, so the business has a heartbeat instead of a constant alarm.

TEMPLATE — A weekly operating rhythm Start of week: review the numbers (sales, new leads, money owed) and pick the one focus for the week. Across the week: deliver client work, your human-kept 20%, every piece through the quality gate. One batch block: run the content engine for the week's posts, and batch your outreach in one sitting. Always running in the background: support FAQs, reminders, checkout, and delivery, automated. End of week: a fifteen-minute review, are the automations still working, and update the tracker. Adapt the days to your life. The point is a rhythm, not a rigid schedule.

Batching is the quiet superpower here. Doing all your content in one block, all your outreach in another, is far faster than scattering them through the week, and it is what lets one person cover the work of several.

The honest limit of a one-person back office

REALITY CHECK "With AI running every function, the business basically runs itself." Not quite, and the gap matters. AI fills the roles, but you are still the single point of judgment and accountability for all of them. It is not a real team that thinks and decides independently. It is a very capable set of tools that still needs an operator pointing them and checking their work. The back office dramatically reduces your load and lets one person do what took many. It does not remove your ownership. If you check out entirely, it drifts, then breaks. Less work, real leverage, but not no work and not no you.

That is not a disappointment, it is the design. You wanted to escape doing every task by hand, and you have. You did not need to escape being the person in charge, which is the part that was always yours and always valuable.

Build it as you need it

One restraint, because it is the over-building trap from earlier in a new place. Do not construct an elaborate five-function back office before your business needs one. Add each function's tooling when the load actually demands it. If support questions are not yet drowning you, you do not need a support system yet. The back office grows with the business. Build the function that is currently eating your time, then the next one when it starts to.

What's next

You can now run a whole business's worth of functions as one person, orchestrating rather than laboring. But right now most of how you run it lives in your head, which means the business still depends entirely on you remembering how everything works. The next step is to get it out of your head and into systems, so the machine is repeatable, reliable, and not trapped behind your memory. That is Chapter 15.

TRY THIS Map your business as functions, using the diagram. For each one, write what AI handles and what you keep, so the judgment line is explicit. Then identify the single function eating the most of your time right now, and build its tooling first: if it is marketing, set up the content engine prompt against one real idea from your work; if it is admin, build the minimal tracker. Finally, sketch your own weekly operating rhythm from the template, fitted to your real life. Save the prompts, the tracker structure, and your rhythm to your System Library. You are no longer doing the work of a team. You are running one.

Chapter 15
Systems and SOPs
(Getting the Business Out of Your Head)

You can run a whole business's worth of functions as one person now. But here is the uncomfortable truth about how you are running them: almost all of it lives in your head. How you onboard a client, how you produce the week's content, how you handle a refund, the exact steps of your delivery, all of it exists as memory and habit, retrieved fresh each time you do the task.

That is a ceiling, and it is a fragility. A business that lives in your head can only ever be as big and as reliable as your memory on a given day. This chapter gets it out of your head and into systems, which is what turns a clever solo operator into something that runs.

Why a business in your head is capped

When the business lives in your memory, you are the bottleneck and the single point of failure. Nothing happens unless you are there, remembering how. You cannot hand any piece to AI or to a future helper, because the instructions exist nowhere outside your skull. Quality drifts, because you do each task a little differently every time depending on your energy and mood. And you cannot improve a process you have never actually named and looked at. This is the real constraint at the top rung, the one Chapter 3 warned about: maintaining and improving the machine. You cannot maintain what is not written down.

PLAIN ENGLISH An SOP, a Standard Operating Procedure, is the written steps for doing a recurring task the same way every time. It is the documented "here is how we do this," so the task no longer has to be figured out fresh, or remembered, or done by you specifically. It just gets followed.

"I'm one person, why do I need SOPs?"

REALITY CHECK "SOPs are corporate bureaucracy. I'm a one-person business, I don't need them." You need them more than a big company does, because you have no team to absorb the chaos when something lives only in one person's head, and that person is you, on every task. SOPs for a solo operator are not bureaucracy. They are how you stop being the bottleneck. The version to avoid is the fifty-page manual nobody reads. The version you want is lean, used, and real: the actual steps for the things you actually repeat. Document what you do often and what would break if you forgot it. Skip the rest.

Here is what a documented system buys a single person, laid against the alternative.

Dimension	In your head	In a system
Consistency	Drifts with your mood and energy	Same quality every time
Speed	Re-decided from scratch each time	Followed, not figured out
Can it run without you	No, you are required	Yes, by AI, a helper, or automation
Your mental load	Heavy, you hold it all	Light, your head is freed for judgment
Can you hand off or sell it	No, it is trapped in you	Yes, it is a transferable asset

KEY IDEA A documented system is the thing you can hand off, the thing you can automate, and the thing that makes the business an asset instead of just your labor. You cannot automate a process you have not defined, so the SOP is not extra work on top of automation. It is the first step of it.

From your head to running on its own

You have actually been doing the first part of this all along.

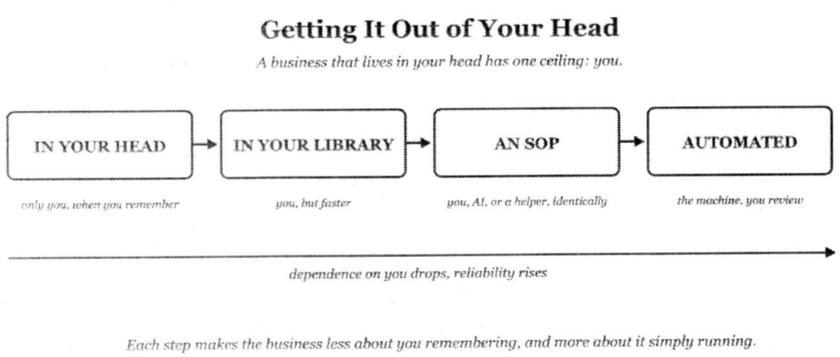

Look at the progression. A task starts in your head, where only you can do it, only when you remember. The System Library you have been building since Chapter 2 was already the first step out: saved briefs and workflows, faster, but still dependent on you. An SOP is the next step: those workflows written up as clear, followable steps that you, an AI, or a future helper could execute identically. And automation, from Chapter 13, is the final step: an SOP wired to run with little or no human touch. Each step to the right makes the business less about you remembering and more about it simply running. The Library, the SOP, and the automation are not three separate projects. They are three stages of the same thing leaving your head.

How to build an SOP, fast

You do not write an SOP from scratch in formal language. You do the task once, brain-dump the steps messily, and let AI turn your mess into a clean procedure.

PROMPT — Turn a brain-dump into an SOP "Here is how I do a recurring task in my business, described messily from memory: [paste your rough notes on the steps]. Turn this into a clean, numbered Standard Operating Procedure that someone else, or an AI, could follow to do it the same way I do, without asking me questions. Include the goal, what is needed to start, the steps in order, and the quality check at the end. Then flag any step that secretly relies on my personal judgment, so I know what cannot be fully handed off."

That last instruction is the important one, and it ties back to the whole Book. The prompt does not just document the task, it surfaces the judgment points hiding inside it, so you keep those human while systematizing everything around them. Use this structure for the result.

TEMPLATE — A working SOP SOP: [task name] GOAL: [the result this produces] RUNS WHEN: [the trigger] NEEDED TO START: [inputs or information required] STEPS:

1. [step]

2. [step]

3. [step] QUALITY CHECK: [how to know it was done right] JUDGMENT POINTS, KEEP HUMAN: [the steps that need a person] LAST REVIEWED: [date]

Then test it the way you tested your product in Chapter 11: could someone follow this with no access to you and reach the result? If there is a gap, you left a step in your head. Close it and the SOP is real.

What to systematize, and what to leave alone

Systematize the repeatable: onboarding, content production, delivery steps, support handling, anything you do the same way more than a few times. Do not try to write an SOP for pure judgment, because you cannot document "have good taste" or "know what this client really needs." But you can, and should, write the SOP for the steps around the judgment. Your delivery SOP does not try to automate the quality gate. It includes "run the quality gate" as a required step, with the judgment kept human inside it. The system holds the procedure. You hold the judgment. That division is the same one running through this entire Book.

Keep them lean and keep them current

Two failure modes to avoid, both familiar. The first is over-documenting: turning a one-person business into a bureaucratic theater of procedures nobody uses. If an SOP is not making something more consistent or freeing your head, it is not earning its place. The second is letting SOPs go stale, the same way automations drift. A procedure written six months ago may describe a tool or a step that has changed. Put your SOPs on the same review rhythm as your automations, the end-of-week check from Chapter 14, so they keep describing reality.

The payoff: a business, not a job

Here is what all this earns you. With your systems documented, the business runs consistently whether you are sharp that day or exhausted. You can hand pieces off, to full automation, to assisted automation, eventually to a person, because the instructions exist outside your head. Your mind is freed from holding every procedure, so it can do the high-value judgment work that is actually yours. And the business becomes a transferable asset, something with value beyond your daily labor, which is the difference between owning a business and being self-employed. That is the top rung becoming real, not a clever person juggling, but a system that runs.

What's next

You are systematizing and automating, which means you are now operating real leverage, and real leverage is where the real dangers live. The next chapter is the one most books in this space refuse to write: the automation traps that quietly wreck the businesses that get this far. Knowing them is what separates the operators who scale from the ones who automate themselves off a cliff. Chapter 16 closes Book Four with the honest warnings.

TRY THIS Pick the single task you repeat most often in your business. Do it once and brain-dump every step, messily, as you go. Run the SOP prompt to turn that mess into a clean procedure, then fill in the SOP template, paying special attention to the judgment points it flags. Test it: could a stranger follow it to the result without asking you anything? Close any gap you find. Then do the same for your next two most-repeated tasks, and save all three SOPs to your System Library. You just moved three pieces of your business from your head to somewhere it can run without you.

Chapter 16
The Automation Traps Nobody Warns You About

Every other book in this space stops at "automate your business" and leaves you there, grinning, in front of a machine you do not yet understand the dangers of. This is the chapter they skip, and it is the one that will save you.

You are now operating real leverage, and real leverage is exactly where the real dangers live. The same automation that multiplies your output multiplies everything else too: your mistakes, your blind spots, your dependence. None of what follows is an argument against automation. It is the judgment that separates the operators who scale from the ones who automate themselves straight off a cliff.

Leverage cuts both ways

Start with the principle underneath every trap in this chapter.

> **KEY IDEA** Automation is leverage, and leverage cuts both ways. The thing that multiplies your good output multiplies your bad output just as efficiently, and it adds costs that do not show up until later. Automate with judgment, task by task, never by default. "Automate everything" is not a strategy. It is how the trap closes.

The most seductive form of this error has its own shape, and you should see it before you walk into it.

The Hidden Cost of Over-Automation

More automation is not always more freedom.

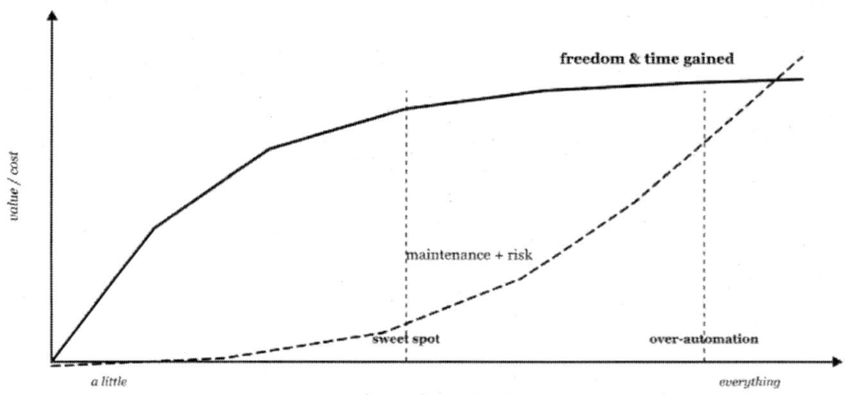

Illustrative. Automation's gift is real, and it has a tail. Stop before the upkeep eats the freedom.

The freedom you gain from automating rises fast at first, because the early targets are the boring, high-value, repetitive tasks, the 80% from Chapter 13. But it plateaus, because there is only so much boring work to remove. Meanwhile the maintenance and risk you take on keeps climbing, and climbs faster the more you automate, because each automation is one more thing to tend and one more place for a silent error to live. Past a certain point, the upkeep curve overtakes the freedom curve, and you have entered over-automation: a person who now spends their days maintaining a sprawl of machines that, together, cost more than they save. The sweet spot is earlier than your enthusiasm wants it to be.

REALITY CHECK "If some automation is good, maximum automation is best." No. More automation is not more freedom past the sweet spot, it is more maintenance, more risk, and more distance from your own business. The goal was never to automate the most. It was to automate the right things and keep the rest human. Measure automation by net freedom gained, not by how much of your business now runs without you.

The six traps

Here are the specific ways automation hurts the businesses that get this far. Learn the warning signs now, because each one announces itself quietly.

The silent failure. An automation breaks or drifts, and because it runs without you, nothing tells you. You discover it when a customer complains about something that has been broken for weeks. The fix is the review rhythm from Chapter 14, plus a simple alert on anything critical, so the system tells you when it stops, instead of a customer telling you.

The scaled mistake. A human doing the wrong thing makes one mistake. An automation doing the wrong thing makes it for every customer it touches, fast, while you sleep. The fix is the judgment line: keep a human checkpoint on anything that goes out to a client or buyer, so a single error cannot reach everyone before a person sees it.

Automating the human edge away. You automate the client emails, then the replies, then the onboarding, and one day a customer realizes they have not interacted with a human once, and they feel it, and they leave. You optimized away the exact thing they were paying a person for. The fix is to automate around the relationship and never the relationship itself.

PLAIN ENGLISH Automation debt is the ongoing cost of everything you have automated: the time spent maintaining it, fixing it when it breaks, and updating it when things change. Every automation you add is an asset and a liability at once. It saves work now and demands upkeep forever.

Automation debt. This is the trap the diagram is really about. Each automation you build is a thing you must now maintain, and a business with too many becomes a full-time job of tending machines. The fix is a hard rule: only automate what clearly saves more than it will cost to maintain, and periodically prune the ones that no longer earn their keep. Fewer, well-chosen automations beat a sprawl.

Going blind. When everything is automated, you stop touching your own business. You no longer read the customer questions, feel the friction, or hear what people actually want, which means you lose the market intelligence that services gave you back in Book Two. You become efficient and blind at the same time. The fix is to stay in deliberate direct contact with some slice of your customers, on purpose, even when you could automate it away, because that contact is how you see what is coming.

Tool dependence. You build your whole operation on one platform's automation, and then it changes its terms, raises its price, breaks an integration, or disappears, and your business breaks with it. The fix is to avoid putting every critical function through a single point of failure, and to keep your core assets, your System Library, your customer relationships, your SOPs, owned by you and portable, not locked inside one tool.

Here is the catalogue at a glance, for when you are reviewing your own setup.

Trap	The warning sign	The fix
Silent failure	You hear about breakage from customers, not yourself	Scheduled reviews plus alerts on critical automations
Scaled mistake	One bad output reaches everyone before you notice	Keep a human checkpoint on anything that ships
Edge automated away	Customers feel they are dealing with a bot	Automate around the relationship, never it
Automation debt	You spend more time tending machines than growing	Automate only what saves more than it costs; prune the rest
Going blind	You no longer know what customers actually want	Stay in direct contact with some customers on purpose
Tool dependence	One tool's change could break the whole business	Keep core assets portable; avoid single points of failure

Check your machines like a skeptic

You cannot fix traps you have not looked for, and the whole danger of automation is that it does not invite you to look. So make the looking deliberate, and make AI play the pessimist.

PROMPT — Automation health check "Here are the automations and systems currently running in my business: [list each, what it does, and when I last checked it]. Acting as a cautious operations reviewer, for each one tell me: how would I know if it silently broke, what would it cost if it produced a wrong output for every user, does it need a human checkpoint it does not currently have, and is it plausibly costing more to maintain than it saves. Then name the single riskiest one and the one most likely to have quietly drifted. Do not reassure me. Find the problems."

Run this on a schedule, not once. The instruction to find problems rather than reassure is the point, because your own instinct, and AI's default, is to assume everything is fine, and "everything is fine" is what every silent failure looks like right up until it does not.

This is pro-judgment, not anti-automation

Do not read this chapter as a reason to retreat. Automation is how you reached a business that runs without you in every step, and that is a genuine achievement worth keeping. The message is narrower and more useful than "automate less." It is: automate with judgment. Automate the boring, high-value, low-risk work. Keep the judgment, the relationships, and the final checks human. Tend what you build, and prune what stops earning. Stay in touch with your own business on purpose. Do that, and automation stays the gift it is supposed to be, instead of curdling into a second job that has quietly taken your customers' trust with it.

The end of Book Four

You now have the whole machine. Services that earn and teach, products that sell on leverage, and automation that lets the business run without you standing in every step, all of it documented in systems and watched with a skeptic's eye. Three rungs, working together, run by an operator who knows what to hand to the machine and what to keep in human hands.

What remains is the question the whole book has been building toward, and the one the title puts right on the cover: how do these pieces stack into something that actually changes your life, and what does that change honestly look like. That is Book Five. Chapter 17 shows how services, products, and automation compound into income that adds up to real freedom, and the chapters after it tell the truth about what that freedom is and is not.

> **TRY THIS** Run the automation health-check prompt on everything currently running in your business, and do not skip the uncomfortable answers. Find your single riskiest automation and do one of two things this week: add the human checkpoint it is missing, or set the alert and review date it needs. Then look at your setup through two of the traps specifically: identify any automation that has quietly put you out of touch with your customers, and pick one slice of customers to start engaging with directly again. Finally, name one automation you built that is not actually earning its maintenance, and consider removing it. Save the health-check prompt to your System Library and put its next run on your calendar.

Chapter 17
Stacking Income Streams That Compound

You have built the whole machine. Services that earn and teach, products that sell on leverage, automation that runs it without you in every step. Book Five is about what happens when those pieces stop being three separate things you do and start being one thing that compounds, because that is where the income on the cover actually comes from.

This chapter is short and it carries one idea worth more than most of the book: stacking is not adding.

Stacking is not adding

The lazy version of this rung is to picture three income streams running side by side, their totals summed at the end of the month. That is addition, and addition is fine, but it is not what you built. What you built is a system where each stream makes the others stronger, and that is multiplication.

> **PLAIN ENGLISH** Compounding is when each gain makes the next gain easier or bigger, so growth feeds on itself instead of just piling up. Adding is one plus one plus one. Compounding is each one making the others worth more.

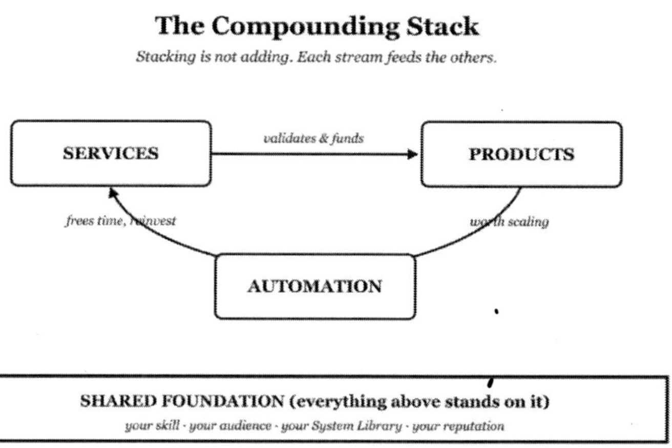

A few connected streams on one foundation compound. Seven scattered hustles just fragment you.

Look at how the rungs feed each other. Your services validate which products to build and throw off the cash to build them, exactly as Chapter 9 showed. Your products, once selling, become proof and content that warm new service leads and reach buyers while you sleep. Your automation frees the time that you pour back into the high-value work, better services, better products. Round and round, each rung handing strength to the next. And underneath all three sits one shared foundation: your skill, your audience, your System Library, your reputation. That shared base is the reason the whole thing compounds, because a gain to the foundation lifts every stream at once. One great testimonial warms your service outreach, sells your product, and seeds your content, all from a single happy client.

KEY IDEA Stack a few connected streams on one shared foundation, and they compound, because each gain lifts all of them. Scatter unrelated income streams, and they only add, while fragmenting the one resource that actually matters: your focus. Depth and connection beat breadth.

The "seven income streams" trap

The gurus love a number. Build seven income streams, they say, as if quantity were the point.

REALITY CHECK "Real wealth comes from having seven income streams." Not when they are seven unrelated things. Seven scattered hustles means seven different skills to maintain, seven audiences to serve, seven things splitting your attention, and none of them feeding the others. That is not leverage, it is self-imposed chaos, and it is the opposite of everything this book taught you about focus and a narrow lane. A few streams that share a foundation and feed each other will out-earn seven disconnected ones, with far less of your life consumed. Do not count your streams. Connect them.

Here is the contrast plainly.

Seven scattered hustles	A stacked, connected few
Split your focus across unrelated things	Share one focus and foundation
Each demands its own skill and audience	All draw on the same skill and audience
Gains stay trapped in one stream	A gain in one lifts all of them
Every new effort starts from zero	Every new effort builds on the System Library

How to stack on purpose

You already built the rungs in order, which was the hard part. Stacking deliberately is mostly about two habits. First, keep all three running rather than abandoning the lower rungs, because the services that feel beneath you once you have products are still your richest source of the next product idea and your freshest market intelligence. Second, look for the feed-points, the specific places one stream can strengthen another, and use them.

PROMPT — Map your feed-points "Here are the income streams in my business: services I offer: [list]; products I sell: [list]; what I have automated: [list]. They all rest on my skill in [lane] and my audience of [buyer]. Show me how each stream could feed the others: what product each service suggests, how each product could generate content or warm leads for the others, and where the time freed by automation is best reinvested. Then name the single strongest connection I am not yet using."

That last line is the valuable one. There is almost always a feed-point you are leaving on the table, a product your repeated service is begging to become, a piece of content your best product could spin off, and naming it is often the highest-return hour you can spend.

The companion habit is where you put the returns. When a stream throws off time, cash, or reputation, reinvest it into the shared foundation, sharpening the skill, growing the audience, thickening the System Library, rather than scattering it into some unrelated new venture. Strengthening the foundation lifts every stream. Starting an unrelated fourth thing just splits you.

The honest part: compounding is slow, then fast

One truth so you do not lose heart. Compounding does not feel like much at first. Early on, when the loops are still thin and the foundation is still young, the streams mostly just add, slowly, and it can feel like a lot of effort for modest return. That is normal, and it is not a sign the model is broken. It is the shape of compounding everywhere: a long, unimpressive beginning, and then an acceleration as the connections multiply and the foundation thickens. The people who quit do so during the slow part, right before the curve turns up. The people who win simply keep feeding the same connected system, patiently, until it starts feeding itself.

What's next

You can now see how the pieces compound into something larger than their sum. Which finally makes it safe to ask the question the cover has been promising and dodging in equal measure: what does the financial freedom at the end of all this actually look like, in honest terms, with no fantasy attached. Chapter 18 answers it straight.

TRY THIS Map your stack. Write out your three rungs and run the feed-points prompt to find how each could strengthen the others, then circle the single strongest connection you are not yet using and make a plan to use it this month. Next, look at whatever your business is currently throwing off, spare time, spare cash, a new testimonial, and choose to reinvest it into your shared foundation rather than into something unrelated. And if you have been tempted to bolt on an unrelated new income stream, ask honestly whether it shares your foundation or just splits your focus. Save your stack map to your System Library and revisit it as the connections grow.

Chapter 18
What Financial Freedom Actually Looks Like

The cover of this book says financial freedom, and I have let the phrase sit there, unexamined, for seventeen chapters. Now I owe you the honest version of it, because the fantasy version, the one the phrase usually sells, will leave you chasing a destination that does not exist while missing the one you can actually reach.

So here it is, straight.

The fantasy and the real thing

The fantasy of financial freedom is infinite money, never working again, a beach, a feeling of having arrived. That is an advertising image, not a destination, and people who chase it either never get there or get there and feel strangely empty, because it was never a real place.

The real thing is more specific and far more valuable: financial freedom is options. It is the point where money stops dictating your choices. That has two sides. There is freedom from, being free of a single boss who controls your income, free of trading every hour for money, free of the low background fear that one bad month ends you. And there is freedom to, being able to choose your work, your hours, who you serve, when to say no, and what to build next. Freedom is not the absence of work. It is the presence of choice.

PLAIN ENGLISH In this book, financial freedom means money no longer dictates your choices. It is measured in options, not in a bank balance. The balance matters only insofar as it buys you the options.

Freedom is a spectrum, not a finish line

Here is the reframe that changes how you experience the whole journey.

The Degrees of Financial Freedom

Freedom is a spectrum, not a finish line.

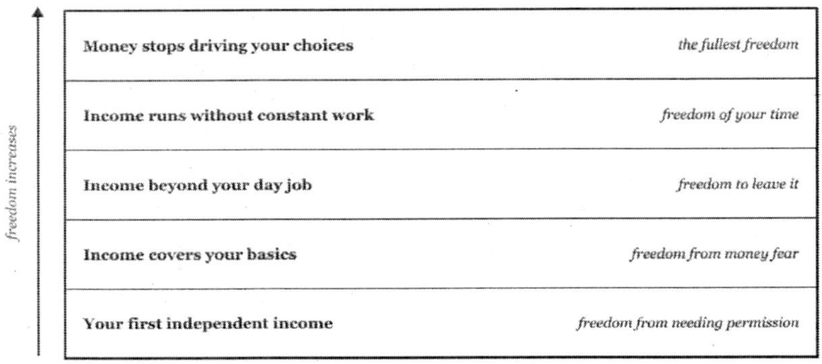

You gain a degree of freedom from the very first dollar. There is no single day you "arrive."

You do not arrive at financial freedom one day, suddenly free where the day before you were not. You gain it in degrees, and you start gaining it from the very first dollar you earn on your own terms. The first time a client pays you instead of a boss, you have won the freedom from needing anyone's permission to earn. When your independent income covers your basics, you have won freedom from immediate money fear. When it grows past your day job, you have won the freedom to leave that job, whether or not you choose to. When it runs without your constant labor, you have won freedom of your time. And somewhere up the ladder, money stops driving your decisions at all. Every one of those is real freedom, available long before any headline number.

KEY IDEA You gain financial freedom in degrees, starting from your first independent dollar, not all at once at some distant finish line. There is no single day you arrive. There is a ladder of freedoms, and you are already climbing it. Notice and value each rung, because each one genuinely changes your life.

The honest truth about "the number"

The title says millionaire, so let me be honest about the number, because the number is where people get lost.

A specific figure is the wrong target, for three reasons. The real goal is what the money lets you do, not the number itself, so aiming at the number aims at the wrong thing. The figure that actually buys freedom is deeply personal, because it depends entirely on your life and your costs, and someone else's number tells you nothing about yours. And chasing a number tends to trap you, because the number recedes: the person who needed one amount to feel free arrives and immediately needs more.

So treat the million on the cover as what it is, an aspirational symbol, a ceiling worth aiming at, not a literal threshold below which you are unfree. Meaningful freedom starts far earlier and is the real prize. Aim at the freedom you actually want, and let the number be whatever delivers that life for you. For some lives that is a large figure. For many it is far less than the fantasy implies, which is good news, because it means freedom is closer than the marketing made it sound.

What freedom is not

REALITY CHECK "I'll finally be free, and happy, when I hit my number." Be careful with that sentence, because it is a trap that has stolen a lot of people's present in exchange for a future that keeps moving. Freedom is not never working, most genuinely free people keep working, by choice, on things they care about. It is not a finish line where contentment switches on permanently, that switch does not exist at any income. And money buys freedom, not fulfillment, which still comes from the ordinary places it always has: people, health, meaning, work you find worth doing. Build the freedom. Just do not outsource your happiness to a future balance, because the freedom is a means, and the life is the point.

The fantasy, beside the real thing

The fantasy of freedom	The real, achievable freedom
Infinite money, never working	Enough that money stops dictating choices
A single moment of arrival	Degrees, gained from the first dollar
One universal number	A personal number, set by your life
Escape from work	Choice over your work

Why the honest version is the better one

None of this should deflate you, because the honest version is the one you can actually reach, and you have already started reaching it. The fantasy pays nothing and recedes forever. The real version pays you in options from the first client, grows as your stack compounds, and is built on something that lasts. You tasted a real degree of freedom the day someone paid you for a result instead of your hours. The rest of the climb is more of that, compounding. That is not a lesser dream. It is the only one that comes true.

Define your own freedom

Generic freedom is unreachable because it is nobody's actual life. Yours is reachable because it is specific. So make it specific.

PROMPT — Define your financial freedom "Help me define what financial freedom actually means for me, specifically, not as a generic dream. Ask me to think through: what I want freedom FROM (a job, a fear, a person, trading all my time), what I want freedom TO do (choose my work, my hours, where I live, who I help), and the rough monthly income that would deliver that life given my real costs. Then reflect back a clear, specific definition of my financial freedom and the income level that would buy it. Finally, point out anything on that list I could start doing now, in some small form, without waiting for the full number."

That last instruction matters most, because a surprising amount of the freedom you want is not actually gated behind the full number. Some of it is available in smaller form today, and seeing that is what keeps the long climb from feeling like deferment of your whole life.

What's next

You know what you are building toward now, honestly, and you can name your own version of it. One thing stands between building it and keeping it: the tools underneath everything you have built will keep changing, fast, and a freedom that depends on today's specific tool is fragile. The next chapter makes your whole system durable, able to outlast any single model or platform, including the one named on this book's cover. Chapter 19 is how you stay ahead of the models.

> **TRY THIS** Run the define-your-freedom prompt and answer it honestly, in specifics, not slogans. Write down your own definition of financial freedom, what you want freedom from and freedom to, and the rough income that would buy that life for you, not for anyone else. Then locate yourself on the degrees ladder: which rung have you already reached, and what is the very next one. Finally, take the prompt's last answer seriously, and pick one piece of the freedom you want that you could start living in some small way this month, without waiting for the full number. The climb is long. The first degrees of freedom are not.

Chapter 19
Staying Ahead of the Models

You know what you are building and what freedom it is meant to buy. One thing stands between building it and keeping it, and it is the speed at which everything underneath you changes. The AI tools you rely on will keep updating, renaming, repricing, and leapfrogging each other, fast, and a business tied tightly to any one of them is a business waiting to be knocked over by an update.

This chapter makes your system durable, so the churn stops being a threat and becomes a tailwind. It is also, I will admit plainly, the chapter that future-proofs this very book.

Churn is the only constant

Let me be honest about the thing the rest of the book has been quietly working around. AI models are released and revised at a pace nothing else in business moves at. The model that is current as you read this will be old soon. Names will change, a number will tick up, prices will shift, features will appear and vanish, and what counts as cutting edge will move under your feet. This is not a temporary phase that will settle down. It is the weather now, and you should plan for it instead of being surprised by it every few months.

This book even names a specific model on its cover and in its examples, and that is deliberate, not an oversight. The point is not which model. The point is the system, and the system is built to outlast whatever the model is called by the time this reaches you.

Build on what doesn't change

Here is the move that makes you churn-proof.

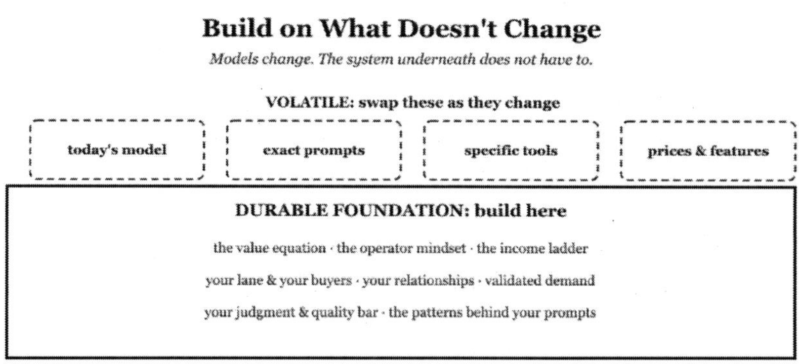

Tie your business to the bedrock, not the blocks on top. Then every new model is a free upgrade.

Everything you work with sorts into two layers. There is a volatile layer that changes constantly: which model is best today, its exact name and version, the precise wording of a prompt, the specific tool or platform, the current prices and features. And there is a durable layer that does not: the value equation from Chapter 1, the operator mindset, the income ladder, knowing your lane and your buyers, your relationships, your validated demand, your judgment and quality bar, and the patterns behind your prompts rather than their exact words.

People who tie their business to the volatile layer get whiplashed by every release. People who build on the durable layer treat each release as a swappable part. The model underneath is just an engine, and you can drop in a newer one whenever a better engine ships, because the thing you built does not depend on the engine's name.

> **KEY IDEA** Build your business on the durable layer, the principles, the relationships, the validated demand, the judgment, and treat the specific model, tools, and prompts as swappable parts on top. What does not change is where you build. What changes is what you swap. Tie yourself to the bedrock, never to the blocks resting on it.

Why updates become good news

Once you have built this way, something nice happens to your relationship with model releases. The person who built their business on one specific model dreads every update, because each one threatens to break what they made. You get the opposite experience. Every new model that is better, faster, or cheaper is a free upgrade to your production engine, and your business quietly gets better or cheaper to run, at no cost to you, because all you did was swap the engine while the system stayed put. You stop fearing the news and start welcoming it.

Built on the tool (fragile)	Built on the system (durable)
A new model drops and you scramble to keep up	A new model drops and you swap it in as an upgrade
A tool raises prices and your margins break	A tool raises prices and you move to another
A tool vanishes and part of your business dies	A tool vanishes and your assets are already portable
The cutting edge moves and you feel left behind	The cutting edge moves and your foundation has not

The habits that keep you durable

A few practical habits keep you on the bedrock. Treat your prompts as patterns, not magic phrases, which is exactly why every prompt in this book was taught with its reasoning attached: a pattern survives a model change, a memorized incantation may not. Do not over-optimize for one model's specific quirks, or you build something that shatters the moment that model changes. Keep your core assets owned and portable, your System Library, your relationships, your audience, your SOPs, rather than locked inside one platform, which is the tool-dependence trap from Chapter 16. Stay loosely aware of major shifts without chasing every release. And when you do adopt a new model, take a few minutes to re-test your key workflows rather than assuming they transfer untouched.

PROMPT: Migrate a workflow to a new model "I built this prompt or workflow on an older model: [paste it]. A newer model is now available. Rewrite it to take advantage of the newer model's strengths while keeping the same goal and the same structure, and then tell me exactly what I should re-test to confirm it still produces the quality I need before I rely on it."

The two opposite traps

Durability has two failure modes, and they pull in opposite directions.

> **REALITY CHECK** "To stay ahead, I need to learn every new model and tool the moment it drops." That is the shiny-object trap, and it is procrastination wearing the costume of progress. If you are always learning the newest tool, you are never earning, and the tool-chasing feels productive while producing nothing. The opposite trap is just as deadly: clinging to one model or platform forever until it changes and breaks you. The answer is neither chase nor cling. Build on the durable layer, swap the tools on top when a clearly better one arrives, and otherwise keep earning. You do not need the newest engine. You need a system that can take whatever engine is best when you happen to look up.

The honest note about this book

By the time you are reading this, the model named on the cover may have a higher number, a new name, or a successor you have already moved to. That is fine, and it is the whole point of this chapter. Nothing in the system you built cares what the model is called. The value equation still holds. The ladder still works. Your lane, your buyers, your relationships, your judgment, all of it is exactly as valid on next year's model as on this one. The cover names a moment. The method outlasts it.

What's next

Your system is durable now, built to survive every update and turn it into an advantage. But durability only matters if you have actually built something, and a plan you never start protects nothing. The final chapter turns everything in this book from understanding into motion, with a concrete plan for your first ninety days. Chapter 20 is where you stop reading and start earning.

TRY THIS Sort your own setup into the two layers. Write down what in your business is volatile, the specific model, tools, and exact prompts, and what is durable, your skill, your buyers, your relationships, your system. Then check the durable side for fragility: are your core assets, your System Library, your audience, your client relationships, owned by you and portable, or trapped inside one tool that could change its terms? Fix any that are trapped. Adopt the habit, starting now, of saving prompts as patterns with their reasoning, not as exact strings. And the next time a model upgrade lands, use the migration prompt to adapt your key workflows instead of either fearing the change or ignoring it.

Chapter 20
Your First 90 Days
(From Reader to Earner)

Everything in this book comes down to what you do in the next hour.

I told you back in Chapter 1 that the thing separating the people who earn from the people who only read is not knowledge. It is action. You now have more system, more method, and more honest guidance than you need. What you do not yet have is a single dollar earned from it, and the only thing standing between you and that dollar is starting. Most people will close this book, feel informed, and do nothing. This chapter exists to make sure you are not one of them.

So here is a concrete plan for your first ninety days, and then the smallest possible first step to take today.

What ninety days is actually for

Let me set the scope honestly, because the hype version of this would promise you an empire by spring.

> **REALITY CHECK** "In 90 days I'll have passive income, products, and an automated business." No. In ninety days of focused work, you get onto the first rung and earn your first real proof: a paying client, cash in hand, a testimonial, a referral. That is the goal, and it is the right one, because it is the foundation everything else is built on and the step that actually changes your self-belief. Products, automation, and the higher rungs come after, on the foundation these ninety days lay. Anyone promising you the whole ladder in a quarter is selling the fantasy this book spent twenty chapters dismantling. Aim for the first rung. It is enough, and it is plenty.

The plan

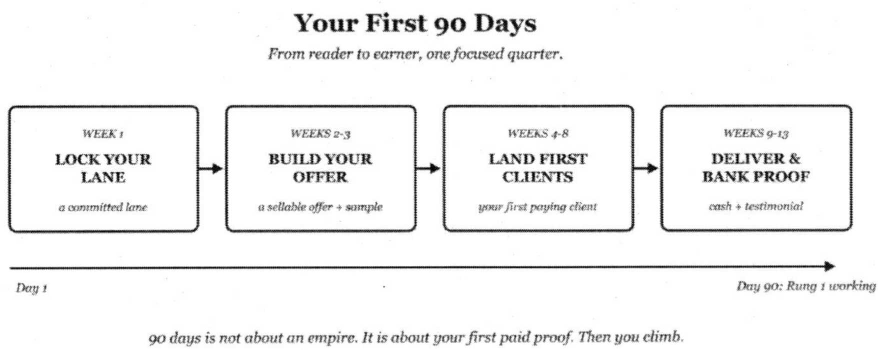

Four phases, mapping exactly to the foundation you have already learned.

Week 1: Lock your lane. Use the three-circle test and the cheap validation from Chapter 4. Run your skills through it, check real demand, produce one sample, and get one signal that someone would pay. By the end of week one you have a committed lane, written as a single sentence: I deliver this result for this buyer.

Weeks 2 to 3: Build your offer. Use the draft and stress-test prompts from Chapter 6. Build the six-part offer, sharpen it to one sentence, and create one strong sample deliverable using the operator's loop. By the end of week three you have a sellable offer and proof you can deliver it.

Weeks 4 to 8: Land your first clients. This is the longest phase because it is the hardest, and it is where most people quit. Use the outreach prompts and templates from Chapter 7. Build your prospect list, start with your warm network, send tailored messages, offer the low-risk free sample, follow up once, and keep going through the silence. By the end of week eight, the goal is your first paying client.

Weeks 9 to 13: Deliver and bank your proof. Use the quality gate from Chapter 8. Deliver through the gate, ask for the testimonial, ask for the referral, and bank the cash. By day ninety you have a working first rung: real income, real proof, and the first entries in your System Library.

That is the whole plan. Nothing in it is new. It is the book, sequenced into a quarter and pointed at a single outcome.

The rules that make it work

A few principles, all of them callbacks, keep the plan on the rails. Stay in one lane with one offer, because focus is what gets you to first cash and scatter is what prevents it. Earn first with services, and do not let the pull toward passive income drag you off the rung that funds everything. Ship before you feel ready, because the polish you are waiting for arrives only after real delivery, never before it. Use AI as your engine and keep the judgment yours, on every deliverable. And above all, be consistent: a little real work every week beats a heroic burst followed by nothing. The plan rewards the person who shows up on week six, not the one who sprinted on week one.

Build your own version

The plan above is the shape. Make it yours, with dates, fitted to the hours you actually have.

PROMPT: Build your personalized 90-day plan "I am starting a one-person, AI-leveraged business and want a concrete 90-day plan to my first paid income. My skills are: [list]. My likely lane is: [lane or candidates]. I can commit about [hours] per week. Build me a week-by-week plan across four phases: lock and validate my lane, build and stress-test my offer, find clients and land the first yes, and deliver and gather proof. For each week give me the specific actions and the output I should have by the end. Keep it realistic for my available hours, and make the goal first paid proof, not a full empire."

TEMPLATE: Your 90-day plan PHASE 1 (Week 1): Lock my lane. By [date], my committed lane is: [result for buyer]. PHASE 2 (Weeks 2-3): Build my offer. By [date], I have: [offer + sample]. PHASE 3 (Weeks 4-8): Find clients. By [date], I have: [first yes or first client]. PHASE 4 (Weeks 9-13): Deliver and bank proof. By [date], I have: [cash + testimonial + referral]. The one thing I will do every single week, no matter what: [your weekly non-negotiable, for example "send ten tailored outreach messages"].

Honest expectations

The truth, as everywhere in this book. Ninety days to first cash is realistic if you do the work consistently, and the first cash will likely be modest, because first cash usually is. Some people will land it sooner, some will take longer than ninety days, and neither means the model failed or that you did. The plan is the path, not a guarantee with a date stamped on it. What you are really after in these ninety days is not a particular number. It is motion and proof: the lived evidence that a stranger will pay you for a result you delivered with a tool you already knew how to use. Once you have that, the doubt that stops most people is gone for good.

Do this now

Plans that start "Monday" tend not to start. So lower the bar to zero and take the first step before you close this book.

> **DO THIS NOW** Take out a blank page and write down three things you can already do that someone, somewhere, pays money for. Just three. That is the entire first action, the same one from Chapter 1, and it is the seed of your lane, your offer, and your first ninety days. You can do it in the next five minutes, and doing it puts you, today, on the earner's side of the line.

The map is done. The walking is yours.

I have given you everything I know: the honest math, the operator's mindset, the ladder, the lane, the offer, the outreach, the delivery, the products, the automation, the systems, the durability, and the honest truth about what freedom is and is not. The map is complete and it is in your hands.

But a map has never moved anyone a single step. The walking is yours, and it always was. Most people who read this far will nod, feel genuinely informed, and never write the three things on the page. A few will. The only difference between those two groups, ninety days from now, is that one of them started.

KEY IDEA You have the complete map. No more reading will move you. The first degree of freedom is one focused quarter away, and it begins with three lines on a blank page. Be the one who writes them.

A Final Word

You came to this book because of a word on the cover, and I want to leave you with the honest truth about that word one more time, because it is the most valuable thing I can give you.

Most books in this aisle sell you a dream and hope you never check whether it was real. I tried to sell you something different: a method, and the truth about it. The truth is that there is no button, no overnight fortune, and no version of this where the money arrives without the work. But the better truth, the one the hype leaves out, is that a single person with a skill, a tool you already know how to use, and the willingness to do the work can now build real income and real freedom, in degrees, starting far sooner than the fantasy ever delivers. That is not a smaller promise. It is the only one that comes true.

I did not write this to impress you with what is possible. I wrote it to hand you something you can actually do. If parts of it were less glamorous than you hoped, that was on purpose, because the glamour is what gets people to buy books and the honesty is what gets them paid.

So here is what I believe, having watched how this actually goes. The people who succeed are almost never the most talented or the most informed. They are the ones who pick one lane, make one offer, send it to one real person, and keep going through the silence until someone says yes. You are entirely capable of being one of them. The only question left is whether you will start, and that question was always going to be yours to answer, not mine.

I am rooting for you. Now go earn the first dollar.

Could You Do Me a Favor?

If this book was useful to you, I have one small ask.

I am an independent author. I do not have a publisher buying ad space or a marketing budget pushing this book in front of people. What I have is readers, and the single most helpful thing a reader can do is leave an honest review. Reviews are how the next person like you, someone with a skill and a quiet hope that this might be real, finds the book and decides to trust it.

It takes a minute, and it genuinely makes the difference for a book like this one. An honest review, whatever you actually thought, is exactly what helps the right readers find it and the wrong ones skip it. That honesty is the whole spirit of the book anyway, so it would be a fitting way to close the loop.

If you would be willing, you can leave your review on the book's page wherever you bought it. Thank you for considering it, and thank you for reading this far.

Your Free Bonus

Everything practical in this book is meant to be used, not just read, so I have put the tools in one place for you.

Your free bonus collects every prompt and template referenced throughout these chapters into a single pack you can copy from directly, instead of flipping back through the book to find them. It also includes the companion resource, which is where the things that change too fast to print live: current rates and pricing benchmarks, current model details, and any tools worth knowing about now. I deliberately kept specific numbers out of the book so it would not go stale the moment a price or a model changed. The companion resource is where those live figures stay current.

If you have not grabbed it yet, get it now, so you have the prompts open beside you while you work through your first ninety days.

Get Your Free E-book

Get Your Free E-book
Scan the QR code below to instantly access the e-book
'The ChatGPT-5 Money Map: Exactly What to Ask AI at Each Stage of Wealth Buildiing', absolutely free

SCAN ME

https://bonus.grapevinebooks.com/aimoneymap